Christians Caught in the

DIVORCE TRAP

Christians Caught in the

DIVORCE TRAP

Helping Families
Recover From Divorce

Bruce Parmenter

COLLEGE PRESS
PUBLISHING COMPANY
Joplin, Missouri

Library of Congress Cataloging-in-Publication Data

Parmenter, Bruce, 1931-
    Christians caught in the divorce trap: helping families recover
from divorce / Bruce Parmenter.
      p. cm.
    Includes bibliographical references.
    ISBN 0-89900-738-4 (pbk.)
    1. Divorce—Religious aspects—Christianity. 2. Divorced
people—Religious life. 3. Divorced people—Pastoral counseling
of. 4. Church work with divorced people. 5. Parmenter, Bruce,
1931- . I. Title.
BT707.P37 1995
248.8'46—dc20   95-18758
                                            CIP

For Ron:
in honor of
Robbie

Table of Contents

Preface

Persons of strict conscience who have been divorced feel trapped between the ideal and the necessary. Since they have a strict conscience, they divorce only when necessary. The same strict conscience seldom grants peace after the divorce. They feel cut off from God and often leave the church.

If you are considering divorce, please take a look at this book before you make your final decision. You are on the verge of one of the most important decisions you will ever make. If you have children, start with the chapter on the children of divorce. Whatever your decision, counsel with yourself one more time by reading this book.

Ministers, church leaders and parents of divorcing children will also find this book helpful. However, I offer a word of caution. When you follow the case of "Peg" and "Pierce," you should be aware that this is not a verbatim report of an actual counseling session. The case is based on the author's counseling experience with many people, but Peg and Pierce are fictitious names. Moreover, the kinds of counselor responses reported here are not actual reports of actual interviews. Some drama is needed to carry the storyline, and I pray that the Holy Spirit will use that story to touch the actual life of some reader.

If you, a minister or elder or therapist, were working

with Peg and Pierce, your responses may have been different than mine. You are welcome to criticize my responses. I have tried to be self-critical in chapter seven.

I chose the mythical Peg and Pierce for two reasons:

1. It is a worst-case scenario. Our feelings correspond to that of Peg's friends. In similar situations, we may be the parents, friend, church member/leader. How do we respond? I needed the difficult situation to dramatize that the grace of God follows us into our worst messes.

2. The Peg and Pierce dilemma fits the theme of this book—Christians who feel trapped. Whether Peg was *actually* trapped is another question, but she felt trapped.

The church has a stake in every marriage, an investment in every family, and feels the impact of every divorce. We are all in it together, for better or for worse. The book will fulfill its purpose if it assists you in confronting the issues and clarifying your thinking. It is my prayer that thoughtful reading of the pages to come will make it a little better.

BRP

Part One:

Christians Caught in the
DIVORCE TRAP

1

The Case of Peg and Pierce

Peg sat in my office, telling me she was married to Pierce, they had two children, and she wanted out of her marriage. Wringing her hands, she described trying to leave Pierce several times but returning each time, dragged back by guilt. With a catch in her voice, she said that she and her husband attended a small faith group which gave strong teachings against divorce.

When I asked Peg why she wanted a divorce she winced at the sound of the word. "The very word 'divorce' tightens my stomach. I feel slightly nauseated and ask myself what I'm doing here considering something which violates my deepest beliefs. But to answer your question, I want out of the marriage because I have never loved Pierce." When I asked how she got into a marriage with a man she does not love, Peg shifted in her chair, lowered her eyes, and said, "Pierce is a good man; he is a good father and a good husband, but I just don't have feelings of love for him and I don't think I ever have."

"We met when we enrolled in a discipleship training group sponsored by our church. It was a small group which met for several weeks of intensive Bible study. Everyone in the group got to be close. Pierce and I paired off, then he began to tell me that he loved me. I couldn't return those feelings, but several Christians in the group said that they felt the Lord was calling Pierce and me into marriage and that we were meant for each other. After awhile I yielded even though my feeling didn't confirm my friends' opinion."

This was not the first time I had watched such a scenario unfold. I asked, "Are you telling me that your friends' suggestions overwhelmed your own feelings and confused you?"

"Yes, that's what happened. I began to doubt my own feelings and started questioning myself. If so many people felt the Lord wanted me to marry Pierce, then perhaps I was wrong, and worse still, maybe I was not listening to the Lord. Certainly, Pierce was a nice guy. I liked him and I respected him, but I did not feel in love with him. But on the other hand, I was young and I was not sure how you were supposed to feel when you were in love, so I laid my doubts on the altar and accepted Pierce's proposal, which incidentally was very romantic with Pierce on his knees offering a beautiful ring with a speech promising undying love and devotion."

"But after the wedding your doubts returned."

She stared out the window. "Well, I now know they never left, but I was able to ignore the sound of their knock on my inner ear. At times it gets so loud that I have to pay attention. I have left Pierce three times intending to divorce, but each time the sounds of guilt were louder than the call to leave."

"And Pierce keeps taking you back?"

"Oh, yes. He not only takes me back, he even tells me that he can accept the fact that I don't love him and that he believes that I will learn to love him. Believe me, I have tried to love him for eight years, but how do you draw on an empty well; how do you give something which is not in you? I feel I'm cheating Pierce of the love he deserves but he's so understanding, so patient, he makes it so hard to leave. Yet to live with him is to commit myself to emotional emptiness. It makes me feel like a shell of a person, just going through the motions of living, without feeling the thrill of touching and being touched by the person you most deeply love. The church has become involved in my problem and everyone tells me I have no 'grounds' to leave my husband and that it would be a terrible sin to divorce him and even worse to marry again. Yet, I am young and I would like to love someone with my whole heart. I'm not in love with another man or having an affair, but I sometimes wonder what it would be like to be married to someone I really love."

I said to Peg, who was now in tears, "You feel trapped in your own marriage?" Quietly she said, "That's exactly the way I feel."

Across thirty years of face-to-face conversation with married people, I have listened to the inner conflict and anguish of several people like Peg. There must be others who would never dare to share their doubt and ambivalence with another person.

Peg also felt theologically trapped, shut off from God. Her interpretation of Scripture on divorce gave her not comfort but condemnation. Few of her acquaintances offered much empathy for her dilemma. Peg was alone and isolated and saw no promise of relief wherever she turned. Her spirituality was diminished and her well-being was in jeopardy.

Questions flock around Peg's problem. Is romantic love necessary for marriage? Why do people allow others to make important decisions for them? Was there some serious emotional deficit in Peg? How is it that Pierce wanted to live with a wife who did not love him? Should people not in love stay married for the sake of the children? Is Peg's dilemma a knot which cannot be untied or is there some way for her to find peace?

Cultural expectations are powerful shapers of marital satisfaction and stability. In the United States and in Western culture generally it is taken for granted that romantic love is the basis for the choice of a marital partner. This expectation creates the reality of the marriage. Therefore persons are less likely to marry unless they feel in love and they are keenly disappointed when romance fades. If persons "fall out of love" or if love does not blossom as expected, they are more likely to divorce, especially in a pluralistic culture where women are upwardly mobile.

When we probe the nature of romantic love; when we ask what it really means; when we are called to define it, we are on difficult grounds, faced with more difficult questions. I cannot give a definitive answer to the question, "What is romantic love?", but I will do better than the popular response of "you will know it when it happens to you!"

Romantic love has many counterfeits, like dependency needs, quirky dynamics such as the need to punish or the need to be punished, or adolescent fantasies.

Healthy romantic love is a mix of sexual attraction, playfulness, shared values, mutual respect, self-respect, flexibility and tolerance, responsible lifestyle, the capacity to receive love as well as give it, shared spirituality, plus a little mystique. Those who are called "behavioral scientists," "clinicians," "therapists," or some such title, tend to discount the "mystique." But they do err. Whether the marriage is made in Tokyo or Toronto, it could use romance! Granted, being in love and loving are not necessarily the same. The former is a feeling and the latter is a behavior. I believe both are required if marriage is to be intimate and mutually rewarding.

That brings us back to Peg. Peg's passivity, her inclination to give in to pressure, her propensity to allow others to make her decisions, had landed her smack in the middle of a marriage which therapists label a "pseudo-marriage." In pseudo-marriages, at least one of the spouses is not in love with the other. This person did not volunteer for the marriage. A pressure group, personal passivity, or a premarital pregnancy corrupted the choice. If a pregnant woman marries for the baby rather than for love, then "the baby made the decision." If she got married because of pressure from friends rather than for love, "her friends made the decision." If a man marries because the woman will enhance his career rather than for love, "a career made the decision."

People may stay in a pseudo-marriage for a lifetime, but such marriages are usually one-sided and non-intimate. In Western culture the hope for such marriages to endure is dim. In marriages made up of persons with strict religious conscience, the prognosis for the marriage to last is fairly good; however, happiness will be severely reduced unless the couple actively and intentionally remake the marriage, building on its strengths and working hard to reduce its weaknesses.

Why did Peg allow others to choose her spouse? Feminists might say "because women are conditioned to be powerless." They have a point, but passive people are found in both genders. Peg was a passive person. Whether she stays in her marriage or leaves, she needs greater confidence in the validity of her own feelings. She may also need to explore the question of whether love is active or passive. Biblical love is active (1 Cor. 13).

Let me explain what I mean when I say, "Biblical love is active." The love described in 1 Corinthians 13 is *"agape,"* the kind of love that is self-giving rather than self-seeking. Peg was highly self-absorbed. She was preoccupied with her feelings rather than her responsibilities. First Corinthians 13 teaches that there is a way to transfer a pseudo relationship into a real one—to kindle our love at the fire of God's love, which then points us away from the love of self and toward the love of neighbor. "We love because He first loved us" 1 John 4:19).

Describing one's marriage as a pseudo relationship can be a cover for narcissistic self-love. In the Greek myth of Narcissus, a young man falls in love with his own reflection in the water. He becomes so enamored of his own beauty that he cannot turn his eyes away, not even to eat. He dies of malnutrition.

The parable of Narcissus tells us that we can die of self-love and that the relationships of the self-absorbed person die also. Death follows the tracks of the narcissistic.

Was Peg such a person? God knows. But active love

can work a miracle. When the spirit of God breaks up the hard core of self-love (Gal. 2:20) a person can begin to ask, "how can I love others?" One can then love others behaviorally, as described in 1 Corinthians 13— "Love is patient, love is kind. It does not envy, it does not boast, it is not proud. It is not rude, it is not self-seeking, it is not easily angered, it keeps no record of wrongs." When one behaves this way, warm feelings are awakened. If we put it into a formula, it would be: Loving behavior = loving feelings.

The narcissistic have the formula backwards. They are not keen on keeping promises. The culture of America feeds narcissism in a thousand ways, but the culture of the Christian Community counters narcissism because at the center of that community stands the cross.

Was there a serious emotional deficit in Peg? Narcissism is a spiritual deficit, a deficiency of the soul, but Peg also suffered from a negative family legacy.

As I came to understand her history, I learned that Peg's self respect was fragile due to living with an alcoholic father and a mother who was highly controlling. Peg lacked trust in her own feelings and belief in her own opinions. Religious as she was, she lacked trust in the goodness of God and possessed little understanding of the nature of Christian selfhood.

How is it that Pierce could live with a wife who did not love him? His self-respect was also low, leaving him feeling he did not have the right to expect much out of the relationship. In addition, Pierce came from a long line of alcoholic family members. He was quite willing to suffer in order to rescue and manage Peg. He was more willing to tell her what she should do than to face how she felt.

Is the dilemma of Peg and Pierce frozen or is there the possibility for a thaw? Is it possible for them to find peace even if they divorce? The answer is "yes," but for people of strict religious conscience like Pierce and Peg, peace is not likely to come unless they can also rethink their theological assumptions about divorce.

Assumptions about divorce may include the belief that there are only two acceptable grounds for divorce, namely, adultery and desertion. Particular groups may add other grounds, but the double grounds for divorce are traditional. This position is based on interpretations of Jesus on adultery and Paul on desertion. My interpretation is also based on statements from Jesus and Paul, words which I had overlooked until recent years.

2

The Most Overlooked
Words of Jesus on Divorce

The most astonishing feature of Jesus' teaching on divorce and remarriage is how little of it there is. Everything He said on the subject is printed below. His words are even more brief when you consider the overlap in these quotations:

> Some Pharisees came to him to test him. They asked, "Is it lawful for a man to divorce his wife for any and every reason?"
>
> "Haven't you read," he replied, "that at the beginning the Creator 'made them male and female,' and said, 'For this reason a man will leave his father and mother and be united to his wife, and the two will become one flesh'? So they are no longer two, but one. Therefore what God has joined together, let man not separate."
>
> "Why then," they asked, "did Moses command that a man give his wife a certificate and send her away?"
>
> Jesus replied, "Moses permitted you to divorce your wives because your hearts were hard. But it was not this way from the beginning. I tell you that anyone

who divorces his wife, except for marital unfaithfulness, and marries another woman commits adultery."

The disciples said to Him, "If this is the situation between a husband and wife, it is better not to marry."

Jesus replied, "Not everyone can accept this word, but only those to whom it has been given. For some are eunuchs because they were born that way; others were made that way by men; and others have renounced marriage because of the kingdom of heaven. The one who can accept this should accept it" (Matt. 19:3-12).

Jesus then left that place and went into the region of Judea and across the Jordan. Again crowds of people came to him, and as was his custom, he taught them.

Some Pharisees came and tested him by asking, "Is it lawful for a man to divorce his wife?"

"What did Moses command you?" he replied.

They said, "Moses permitted a man to write a certificate of divorce and send her away."

"It was because your hearts were hard that Moses wrote you this law," Jesus replied. "But at the beginning of creation God 'made them male and female.' 'For this reason a man will leave his father and mother and be united to his wife, and the two will become one flesh.' So they are no longer two, but one. Therefore what God has joined together, let man not separate."

When they were in the house again, the disciples asked Jesus about this. He answered, "Anyone who divorces his wife and marries another woman commits adultery against her. And if she divorces her husband and marries another man, she commits adultery" (Mark 10:1-12).

"Anyone who divorces his wife and marries another woman commits adultery, and the man who marries a divorced woman commits adultery" (Luke 16:18).

"It has been said, 'Anyone who divorces his wife must give her a certificate of divorce.' But I tell you that anyone who divorces his wife, except for marital unfaithfulness, causes her to become an adulteress, and anyone who marries the divorced woman commits adultery" (Matt. 5:31, 32).

I have often wished that Jesus had said more. As a marital therapist for thirty years, trying to work my way through the tangled thicket of family problems, I could have used a textbook on marriage and divorce and remarriage, written by Jesus of Nazareth!

But, on second thought, I am glad He didn't write a textbook, for two reasons: 1. To cover every case and discuss every problem, the text would have been bigger than the New York City telephone directory. 2. However thorough, some would wish that He had said more!

Jesus is Lord of the Christian conscience; therefore, whatever He said on divorce or any other subject, however brief His remarks, carries the heaviest weight. However, Jesus wrote no textbook, and He did not cover all the problems in the game of divorce.

What Jesus did say is plain enough, but we must build a bridge of interpretation from His words to the complex divorce problems that He did not address. I hang on every word that Jesus uttered, but He did not mean for me to hang myself on words He never said! I have talked to so many Christians struggling with divorce that I know they hang themselves on words that Jesus never said, or on words that He did say which are ripped from their context.

So what did Jesus say about divorce? The following is my interpretation (does anyone have anything to offer but an interpretation?) of the bone and marrow of the principles arising from His pronouncements on divorce:

1. Men and women are made in God's image.

2. Married people are "one flesh."

3. God joins people in marriage; man is not to separate them.

4. Moses permitted a certificate of divorce, but this did not represent God's original intent for marriage.

5. If a man divorces his wife, except for her sexual unfaithfulness, he causes her to commit adultery; he commits adultery also when he remarries.

6. Not everyone can accept this teaching, but only those to whom it has been given.

7. The one who can accept it should accept it.

8. A man who marries a divorced woman commits adultery.

I believe that the above eight points represent the essence and the sum of what Jesus said about divorce. Of course, these statements are subject to interpretation and have, in fact, been hashed over, ad nauseum. Scholars have overexamined every word and phrase, literalists have made them into inflexible laws, and liberals have pulled the teeth from these teachings. I believe the words are neither a straitjacket nor grounds for easy divorce.

Nor can the words be separated from their context. The background is explained very well in the following quote from *Cruden's Concordance*:

> The school of Shammah, who lived a little before our Savior, taught that a man could not lawfully be divorced from his wife, unless he had found her guilty of some action which was really infamous, and

contrary to the rules of virtue. But the school of Hillel, who was Shammah's disciple, taught on the contrary, that the least reasons were sufficient to authorize a man to put away his wife; if she did not cook food well, or if he found any woman whom he liked better.

The Pharisees attempted to trap our Lord into some statement with which they could take issue, but He declined to interpret Moses' words, though he declared that he regarded all lesser causes than fornication as standing on too weak ground.[1]

These rabbis, Shammah (Shammai) and Hillel, were polarized in their interpretation of the key passage in Deuteronomy 24:1, "a woman who becomes displeasing to him because he finds something indecent about her." The crunch word is "indecent." Shammai said it meant sexual indecency, that is, adultery. Hillel said indecency means whatever the husband said it means. The Pharisees wanted to discredit Jesus, so therefore gave Him a question which would expose Him to the scorn of one party or the other. Jesus took a position which was conservative, but not legalistic or rigid. Some would argue that Jesus took an approach to the issue, without taking a position. Neither those who trivialize marriage nor those who would fashion marriage into a legalistic trap are supported by Jesus' teachings. Divorce is usually a tragedy, a very hurtful experience to spouses, and especially to children. But divorce need not be an ultimate tragedy.

Someone said, "The difference between a problem and a mess is that a problem can be fixed but a mess has

---

1. Alexander Cruden, *Cruden's Complete Concordance* (Philadelphia: C. Winston Company, 1949).

to be redeemed." Divorce is usually a mess rather than a problem, but a mess which can be redeemed. "Redemption" is a theological word standing for a spiritual experience. The prerequisites of redemption are repentance and forgiveness. Repentance and forgiveness are empty words unless they flow from the cross and resurrection of Christ.

Usually divorce is a mess requiring redemption, but in certain cases it is a liberating experience. Some marriages are so bad that they should and must be ended. Some divorces are good and righteous altogether. Some marriages are evil, not because they split, but because they remain intact. When children are verbally, physically, and sexually abused by one of their parents, and that parent shows no intention to repent and no willingness to seek therapy, the other parent does a good thing to divorce. To remain in the marriage would be evil.

Cruden's statement that Jesus' regarded all lesser causes than fornication as "standing on too weak ground" is accurate. But child abuse, substance abuse, withdrawal of affection, dominance, and other hurtful acts, both active and passive, certainly are not "lesser grounds than fornication." Many a marriage has survived an isolated act of infidelity, hurtful as it is, but marriage must not provide a shelter for abuse.

The disciples of Jesus found His teachings on marriage and divorce to be so lofty and demanding, that they told Him in private, "If this is the situation . . . it is better not to marry." His reply, in private and free from the trap posed by the Pharisees, was this: "not everyone can accept this teaching, but only those to whom it has been given. For some are eunuchs because they were born that way; others were made that way by men; and others have renounced marriage because of the kingdom of heaven. The one who can accept this should accept it." This statement made in private to His disciples certainly softens His words made in public to the Pharisees. Yet, the public words have been given greater emphasis, which means that legalistic Christians have been controlled by the Pharisees more than they have been controlled by Jesus.

The new Moses takes essentially the same position as the first Moses: some concession has to be made to the limits of human nature. Compassion rises above the rules. Mercy transcends law.

Yes, it is true that we hear what we want to hear and that we are deaf to words that do not fit our presuppositions. Legalists do not want to hear the words, "Not everyone can accept this teaching, but only those to whom it is given . . . the one who can accept this should accept it." At the very least, these words mean that the Lord is tolerant of those who do not live up to His ideals for marriage. They surely mean that though divorce and remarriage breach God's will, they do not place repentant and grace-seeking divorced people outside the kingdom.

William Barclay told the story of how two English soldiers carried the body of their buddy from a World War I battlefield to a nearby church cemetery. At dusk, they knocked on the door of the rectory. When the priest came to the door, they asked permission to bury the body of their friend in the church graveyard. The priest asked if their buddy were of the Catholic faith. They replied that he was not. The priest said, "The cemetery is consecrated ground. I cannot permit burial if your friend is not Catholic. I am sorry." The soldiers went away, but stopped at the edge of the cemetery, dug a shallow grave, and buried their friend just outside the fence.

The next morning they returned to examine the gravesite and pay their respects before they moved on. To their surprise, they could not locate the grave. As they were searching, the priest appeared. He explained: "I could not sleep. My conscience bothered me. In the middle of the night I got up and went out and moved the fence. Here is the grave of your friend, just inside the fence."[2]

The church has its rules. They are there for a reason—to protect the sacred. But human personality is also sacred. When the rules got in the way of redeeming a person, Jesus eased the rules. He said, "The Sabbath (the rule) was made for human beings, not human beings for the Sabbath."

Consider this question, "Is it lawful for a man to divorce his wife for any and every reason?" Jesus replied, "Haven't you read that at the beginning the Creator made them male and female?" *This response struck right at the heart of the oppressive male chauvinism of the Pharisees and rejected it in the strongest possible terms.* Note the question: "Is it lawful for a man to divorce his wife . . . ?" In the Jewish culture of Jesus' time a woman did not have the option of divorcing her husband. *Jesus' answer is a strike at male dominance, control, and oppression of women.* He will not have it. Men are not allowed to "thingify" women. They also are made in the image of

---

2. The story is attributed to William Barclay, but I am unable to verify the exact source.

God, possessing equal status with men. Jesus' words, "I tell you that anyone who divorces his wife, except for marital unfaithfulness, and marries another woman, commits adultery," holds men responsible for what they do to their wives and protects the dignity of womanhood.

The statement, "Some are eunuchs because they were born that way; others were made that way by men; and others have renounced marriage because of the kingdom of heaven," is one of the most fascinating that Jesus ever made. But what does it have to do with divorce and remarriage? Everything. At least two major implications for the problem of divorce and remarriage are found here. Both are redemptive for those hurt by broken marriages.

1. The language about "eunuchs" (castrated males) is a concession to the sexual needs of divorced people. "Eunuchs" can live with the ideal teaching against remarriage because a eunuch has no sexual drive. "Others" who "have renounced marriage—because of the kingdom of heaven," probably refers to those who have chosen celibacy as a lifestyle and who have disciplined themselves to abstain from sexual activity. Such persons are exceptions to those with usual sexual needs and behavior. Most people cannot "accept" (read "live with") the hard teachings on celibacy, especially those who have become conditioned to sexual gratification in previous marriages. As one of my clients said, "I am neither a eunuch nor a saint." If Jesus' teachings were not tempered to such persons, then He would be guilty of the same charge He made to the Pharisees: "They tie up heavy loads and put them on men's shoulders, but they themselves are not willing to lift a finger to move

them" (Matt. 23:4). Jesus compassionately and realistically tempered his teachings to those with strong sexual needs. Paul followed his master with the statement, "It is better to marry than to burn with passion" (1 Cor. 7:9).

2. The phrase "Others were made that way (eunuchs) by men," pointed to gross violence in the culture of Jesus' time. Male slaves were castrated in order to remove sexual threats from those they served. It was a violently depersonalizing act, much akin to the violence done to women divorced by men. Such women were virtually forced into prostitution as a means of survival. I believe this is what Jesus had in mind when He said, "Anyone who divorces his wife, except for marital unfaithfulness, causes her to become an adulteress." By analogy, those who are forced into celibacy by a harsh interpretation of Jesus' divorce teachings have been treated violently.

Nevertheless, the main thrust of the "eunuch" language is—Jesus acknowledges that, by virtue of sexual needs, most divorced persons will not and cannot remain divorced. Jesus can never be seen as a legalist without doing violence to the Gospel portrait of His personality; there is no reason to assume that He would not honor non-sexual needs such as companionship, financial security, or the need to have a father or mother for one's children.

Through Christian history, the church has often hedged these rules when caught between the polarities of literal adherence to certain sayings of Jesus and compassion for people caught in the quagmire of actual divorce cases.

The church father, Origen, raised the question: what if a husband returns from a trip to find his wife has killed the children? Does he have "grounds" for divorce? She was not sexually unfaithful. All she did was murder the kids! Origen's question was rhetorical, but it highlights the dilemma created by a literalistic, unbending interpretation of Jesus' words on divorce.

On the other hand, those who flit in and out of marriage like barn swallows find no support in Jesus' words. Marriage is sacred. Stick with it; make it work; leave no stone unturned to enrich and preserve it. Be faithful to your spouse, but be gracious as well. Don't leave your marriage until you have done everything in your power to make a go of it.

When it fails, know that you are no less loved, no less valued, and no less in the kingdom. Accept responsibility for your part in the marital failure, receive God's forgiveness and healing, learn what you can from the brokenness, and get on with your life.

> O how I wish there were
> some wonderful place
> called the Land of Beginning Again,
> where all our heartaches
> and all our mistakes
> could be dropped
> like a shabby old coat
> at the door
> and never put on again.
> —Author Unknown

There is, my divorced friend, "a land of beginning again."

3

The Most Overlooked
Words of Paul on Divorce

What follows is a fresh interpretation of Paul's teachings on divorce. I say "fresh" because this interpretation is seldom heard in conservative circles.

In preparation for this chapter, the reader is encouraged first to read the entire seventh chapter of 1 Corinthians. This is the only place in Paul's writings where he discusses divorce in any detail.

Paul's discussion in 1 Corinthians 7 is a pastoral response to specific questions. He opens the chapter with the phrase: "Now for the matters you wrote about." This expression appears six times in Paul's writings and each time he is taking up a specific question. This time he is responding to questions about marriage.

Paul, like Jesus, does not offer a systematic treatment of marriage and divorce. He does not give a complete treatment of the ethics of divorce, a thorough discussion of most facets of the problem. Like Jesus, he does not deal with such issues as domestic violence, radical discrepancy in intimacy needs or alcoholism.

Paul was not asked these questions. We are left with the task of trying to understand what Paul did say and of trying to relate that to the problem of marriage, divorce, and remarriage in the contemporary world.

The problem posed for us by the scanty biblical teachings on divorce was also a problem for Paul. The Corinthian correspondence confronts Paul with a new situation, an ethical problem on which Jesus had not spoken.

The problem arose out of the context of Paul's missionary work. The problem posed in one of the questions to Paul was: When one spouse only was converted to Christ should that spouse stay with her husband, or should she divorce him? (The question arose in the Gentile world where women had the power of divorce.) A corollary question: What about the children: if one parent is an unbeliever, are the children "unclean" (probably a reference to the possibility that some members of the church might consider the marriage of a believer to an unbeliever illegitimate, and the children thus illegitimate)?

On this question, Paul had no word from Jesus. On many of the marital and family situations facing the modern church, we have no word either from Jesus or Paul. As the centuries rolled by, the church was confronted with ethical questions never before faced. The brief comments of Jesus and Paul on divorce do not address every new question. We are frequently left to arrive at our conclusions on the basis of assumptions about what the Lord would have us to do.

Paul shared this dilemma, for Jesus made no comment on the problem posed by a believer married to an unbeliever. If Paul had been a legalist, he would have said nothing because Jesus was silent on this new situation. To say nothing would have "shut the Kingdom of God in men's faces," precisely because it would have left them with no pastoral guidance. The result would have been confusion and despair with the strong possibility of defection from the church. Paul spoke where Jesus did not speak, but he did so out of deep pastoral concern.

Paul responds to the questions asked by Christians in Corinth in the light of three overarching themes: (1) Marriage is good, but due to "the present crisis" and since "the time is short," proposed marriages would best be deferred. If possible, "remain as you are." (2) Whatever you do, do it "in the Lord." (3) "God has called us to live in peace." None of these themes is treated in a legalistic manner.

Paul first addresses a question about the unmarried (never-married) and widows (1 Cor. 7:8-9). His response: it is good to remain unmarried, but marry if you must. The "must" is shaped by the reality of strong sexual passion. Like Jesus, Paul balances idealism and realism. Like Jesus, Paul acknowledges the "given" of sexual need and makes concession to that need. The "concession" is not made out of grudging compromise of the "higher" spiritual nature to the "lower" fleshly nature. Such a position would reflect Greek or Gnostic assumptions. Paul thinks like a Hebrew rather than a Greek. Greek Gnosticism considered flesh to be evil. Hebrew thought did not regard the body as evil. Hebrew thought locates evil in the will and psyche rather than in the body. For Hebrew thought, the body is good because God created it. Sexual need and sexual gratification are good since God created our sexuality.

Sexual expression must be experienced, however, within the context of marriage. Paul's words are conditioned by "the present crisis." We do not know the nature of this crisis, but it was severe enough for Paul to say it is better, now, to remain unmarried. But he held that if Christians found celibacy to be extremely difficult, their personal needs would transcend his advice.

Before taking up additional questions, Paul repeats the ideal for marriage as given by Jesus (10,11). If Paul had taken the words of Jesus as an unbending rule, his discussion of divorce would have ended at this point. That he did not is made clear by his statements in verses 15, 27 and 28.

Paul's reminder of the ideal acknowledges that married people may find it necessary to separate. His statements, "If she does, she must remain unmarried or else be reconciled to her husband" and "A husband must not divorce his wife," are consistent with Jesus' teaching that unless people have good reason for divorce, they sin in divorce and remarriage. (Nowhere in Jesus or Paul, however, is such sin judged to be unforgivable.)

Paul's handling of the next question on the situation of the believer married to the unbeliever is introduced by the phrase, "I, not the Lord." This phrase acknowledges the silence of Jesus on such cases, and lets us know that what is coming is Paul's opinion, an opinion which is given by one "who by the Lord's mercy is trustworthy," and one who "has the Spirit of God," but which is not based upon direct statements from Jesus. (Therapists, ministers, and others working with the divorced or divorcing would do well to speak with similar humility.)

Paul's advice is that believers should not divorce unbelievers, but if the *unbeliever* leaves the marriage, the believing man or woman is "not bound." Most interpreters of this phrase, as do I, hold that the phrase "not bound" gives permission for the believer to remarry. If they must remain single, they would be "bound." If this interpretation is correct, the language of verse nine and the latter half of verse thirty-nine, although not directed at the subject of divorce, would also be appropriate for the believing spouse whose unbelieving spouse has left the marriage. "But if they cannot control themselves, they should marry, for it is better to marry than to burn with passion," and "She is free to marry anyone she wishes, but he must belong to the Lord."

In sum, a believer must make every effort to keep the marriage intact (16), but if the unbeliever wants out, the believer does not incur guilt and may remarry a believer. If the unbeliever is willing to live with the believer, the children are not illegitimate (14).

Paul then takes up the question of the non-married and gives a brief response consistent with his previous remarks: remain unmarried if possible (25-27). The reverse of this statement is consistent with Paul's main thrust; remain married if possible, but if marriage is impossible, remain a divorced person if possible. If that is impossible, marry again "in the Lord," and then live at peace, with yourself, with your "ex," and with the Lord.

The NIV makes a paragraph out of verses 25-28, presumably on the assumption that Paul's discussion in verses 25-28 is about virgins. This is a mistake. Paul, in this section, is discussing both virgins and the divorced. The NIV committee, of course, knows that paragraphs and chapter headings are arbitrary, since the Greek text has none. What they may not so readily acknowledge is that paragraph arrangements may reflect the interpretive bias of the given translator. That is the case in the NIV rendering of verses 25 through 28, particularly verse 27. NIV translates verse 27 as follows: "Are you married? Do not seek a divorce. Are you unmarried? Do not look for a wife." The NIV arbitrarily translates the same word, (λύσιν, lusin) differently in these two lines. There is no warrant for this. This is what Paul said in verses 27 and 28: "Are you married? Do not seek a release (divorce). Are you released (divorced)? Do not look for a wife. *But if you do marry, you have not sinned*" (emphasis mine). The immediate antecedent of "if you do marry" is the divorced, not the never-married. The statement is quite clear; *Paul is saying that divorced people can remarry without sinning*. Who are these divorced? The text does not yield certainty on that question, but they are probably the persons discussed in verses 12-16, namely believers who were divorced by their unbelieving spouses. In any case, Paul's general position is this: if you have sufficient reason to divorce, you have sufficient reason to remarry. If you remarry, it should be "in the Lord" (to another Christian). Your goal is peace. The rendering of verse 27 in the NIV is not accurate. It is ironic that the King James Version of verses 27 and 28 is much closer to the original: "Art thou bound unto a wife? Seek not to be loosed. Art thou loosed from a wife? Seek not a wife. But and if thou marry, thou hast not sinned." The KJV is virtually a literal translation of the Greek text. The NIV handling of these verses is yet another example of how translators can read their beliefs into the text.

Paul's flat-out statement that the divorced may marry again without sinning has never been widely acknowledged. I had been teaching and preaching the Bible for twenty-five years before I became aware of this verse. I first resisted the possibility that Paul gave permission to the divorced to marry again. After reading the passage again and again, I could no longer miss the point that Paul taught that the divorced could marry again without sinning.

At first reading, Paul's statement, "Are you divorced from a wife? Seek not a wife. But if you marry, you have not sinned," seems to contradict his quotation of Jesus in verses 10 and 11: "to the married I give this command (not I, but the Lord): a wife must not separate from her husband. But if she does, she must remain unmarried or else be reconciled to her husband."

The keys to resolving the contradiction are in the phrases: "not I, but the Lord" and "I, not the Lord." In the first instance, Paul is quoting the ideal for marriage as stated by Jesus. In the second instance Paul, knowing that Jesus did not address in detail the many ethical questions of divorce, spoke into the silence. Paul's pastoral concern found it necessary to speak where Jesus had not spoken, to speak what he felt best approximated the redemptive love of Jesus for hurting persons. His permission for the divorced to remarry would, of course, be conditioned by the general qualifications found in the chapter: (1) Since Paul believed the Lord would come soon he advised people not to change their life situation. Nevertheless, if they must, they may marry or remarry. (2) If they do so, it should be "in the Lord," that is, to a fellow Christian. (3) God has called us to seek peace in every life role and style, in every circumstance, in every relationship. It is important to keep marriages together, but it is more important to keep the peace. It is true that most divorces do not bring peace, but some do. Life with a new marital partner may be no more peaceful than life with the first (especially if one learned nothing from the divorce), but sometimes it is.

People should work hard to resolve marital conflict. When resolution is impossible, let them depart in peace. "God has called us to live in peace." This short but potent statement conditions Paul's advice on divorce. The phrase is a description of God's will for any married person, whether previously divorced or not. We are called to peaceful lives in or out of marriage, but it is a *peaceful* marriage rather than avoidance of divorce which is the goal of a Christian marriage. Divorce may not guarantee the enjoyment of peace, but the Christian commitment to peace must be one of the values at work in the decision to remain married or be divorced. "Blessed are the peacemakers, for they will be called children of God" (Matt. 5:9).

Paul's approach to divorce is in the same spirit as that of Jesus. Both balance idealism and realism. Both set forth an extremely high view of marriage, applied to the actual human situation humanely and flexibly. Both use a "case" approach to marriage rather than a systematic approach. Each responds to specific questions. Neither sets out to give a thoroughgoing discussion of divorce. Both affirm the essential goodness of human sexuality and both recognize that the power of sexual and intimacy needs will mean that remarriage may be better than remaining single (Matt. 19:11; 1 Cor. 7:27, 28). Both Jesus and Paul teach that those who have sinned in divorcing can be forgiven and restored to health.

The foregoing interpretations of Jesus and Paul on divorce have included the point that a person incurs guilt in divorcing unless that person has a "grave" or "compelling" reason for the divorce. I am aware that my language is also vulnerable to legalistic rationalization and self-justification. If a person wants out of a marriage, for whatever reason, he is usually able to find "grave" faults in the spouse. I assume that there are few guiltless divorcing or divorced persons. I am convinced that some can be found, but their cases are rare. I am equally convinced that, in most cases, no marriage counselor, minister, attorney, divorce mediator, family member, friend, or anyone else has exact knowledge of the true identity of the guilty or guiltless. Even if we did, we would be prone to forget the words of Jesus, "Let him who is without sin among you be the first to cast a stone at her."

What is a "grave" or "compelling" reason for divorce? Only those whose marriages are in crisis can give the final word, for those persons alone know what it is like to be married to his or her particular spouse. It is not for those standing *outside* the marriage to presume to know how much those *inside* the marriage can bear. Therefore, the decision to divorce is a lonely one, even when the divorcing have sought the counsel of trusted friends or professionals. The divorcing are saying to their friends, family, and professional consultants: I *know* I am the one who must make this decision, but stay alongside me as I make it. Do not desert me, do not leave me alone, for now I need your support. Remaining "alongside" people in marital crisis is the ministry of the Holy Spirit for He is the Paraclete, the One who "comes alongside us."

Yet, the Holy Spirit is the Confronter as well as the Comforter. He is the Spirit of truth as well as the mediator of consolation. The high ideals for marriage in the words of Jesus and Paul are there to remind us that marriage is a commitment as well as a source of personal gratification. Marriage is a relationship where the first commitment of the Christian is a commitment to the Lord to meet the needs of the spouse (1 Cor. 13:5; Eph. 5:21; Phil. 2:4). It is true that if your spouse does not share this commitment, your own needs will not be met. It is difficult to satisfy the basic needs of your spouse when your own basic needs are not satisfied. Marriage lives and moves and has its being in the delicate interplay of a mutual need-fulfilling relationship. The need-fulfilling system of marriage is nurtured by commitment, but commitment must in turn be nurtured by persons who possess the capacity to meet needs. (The Holy Spirit calls the married to be need-meeting persons.) Failures in marriages are located where needs go unmet. Those who have the capacity to meet authentic needs but fail to do so are the persons responsible for the failure of a marriage, whatever the *apparent* "cause" may be.

Even when the Holy Spirit tells a divorced person that they were responsible in some way for the demise of the marriage, that same Spirit also calls that person to repentance and to the reception of mercy and healing. Repentance is the acceptance of responsibility for destructive behavior together with the determination to seek God's help in making necessary changes.

Healing is possible when repentance embraces

awareness that grace includes forgiveness of all failure and acceptance by the God who never sees the label "divorced."

Let this chapter come to a close with the words of Augustine: "Let those who think I have said too little, or those who think I have said too much forgive me. Let those who think I have said just enough, join me in giving thanks to God."

4

No Decision Is a Decision

For forty-five minutes Peg and I had discussed the main features of divorce in the words of Jesus and Paul.

P: This is all so new to me. I have never heard anything like that before. In fact, I didn't know those verses were in the Bible.

B: Join the club. I overlooked them until about fifteen years ago, and I am fifty-eight.

P: How did you finally become aware of these verses?

B: A good friend helped me. His credentials as an interpreter of the New Testament were far better than mine. In fact, his scholarship is world class. Yet, it wasn't like being overwhelmed by superior scholarship. New insight arose out of many hours of quiet dialogue. His office was across the hall from mine in the seminary. He taught Greek and Biblical Studies. I taught Pastoral Care and Counseling. On fall weekends, we would call the dogs and go quail hunting. We roamed the hills of western Illinois in search of the wily quail.

The crisp November air was in our nostrils and theology was in our conversation. We were really there for the companionship and the excitement of conversation on important ideas and feelings. Few experiences surpass the spiritual stimulation and mental clarification of philosophical dialogue between two good friends. Little did we know at the time that one of us would pass through the turbulence of divorce. It is one thing to probe the subject of divorce intellectually, yet another to experience divorce personally.

Our friendship evolved into the development of an elective class, which we taught as a team, on "Divorce and Remarriage." We asked our students to write papers clarifying their own theology of divorce. The classes were filled with intense, exciting and heated discussions. The class was popular with students, yet at times it wrenched our guts and blew our minds. Many of the students were serving weekend ministries and some of them were deep in the pastoral care of people threatened by divorce. Several students had lived through the trauma of their parents' divorce. Others were hip-deep in their own marital conflict. My own theology was probed on every side. In addition, my private practice exposed me daily to clients in every stage of divorce and remarriage. Theology shapes life and life shapes theology, but that theology which is least in touch with life is more likely to be frozen into rules and codes.

Forgive me for such a long speech, Peg (to do so violates all the rules of good therapy), but let me add this: people who talk about "grounds" for divorce are not speaking the language of Jesus. They are recycling the talk of law and legalism. When we use the word "grounds" we have left the seminary and moved across the street to the law school. The Pharisees approached Jesus with this opening line: "Is it lawful for a man to divorce his wife for any and every reason?" They were lawyers. They thought like lawyers and used the jargon of lawyers. Jesus was a pastoral theologian. He was interested in helping people enter the kingdom of God. He said that He came that we might have life and have it to the full. He was not interested in grounds, He was interested in grace.

When people ask what are the grounds for divorce in the New Testament, or what are the biblical grounds for divorce, they are asking the wrong question. To ask that question is to ask the lawyer rather than to ask Jesus. If anything can be said to be known of Jesus without a shadow of a doubt, it is this: He was not a legalist. He always put people ahead of the rules. He said, "The Sabbath is made for man (persons) rather than man (persons) for the Sabbath." He forgave an adulterous woman, setting aside the law requiring her death by stoning. He said, "The Lord requires mercy rather than sacrifice."

Jesus was a shepherd of souls, not a legalist, and that means He lived on the borderland between Scripture and experience, between salvation and suffering. He never once sacrificed a human being to a "bare and bony" rule. "Grounds" was not in his vocabulary. When we study Jesus on divorce, it is not enough to look at His words; we must also look at His deeds. His words and deeds are congruent. They embody compassion. He understands the complexity and ambiguity of the human situation, and is interested in looking forward rather than backward. For Him, the past was important because it needed to be probed for pockets of unforgiven, unhealed, and unredeemed guilt and hurt. With the trauma isolated, He was ready to say, "Neither do I condemn you, go and sin no more." I'm sorry, Peg, for such a long sermon. I guess I ought to pass the offering plate and let you go home.

P: Don't pronounce the benediction yet. I want to respond to what you said. It sounds good and what you've said makes me feel better, but I know I won't be in my bed tonight before I have a thousand doubts. In fact, I feel them crowding in now. For one thing, you know I'm a passive person; I could cave in to your persuasion just as I yielded to the opinions of my friends who thought I ought to marry Pierce. I need to think this through for myself; I need to settle my own mind. This time I need to make my own decision.

B: I couldn't agree more. In fact, I would caution you against a quick shift in your thinking. A pseudo-theology is no better than a pseudo-marriage.

P: I feel trapped between an empty marriage and the fear of divorce, caught in the guilt of not being able to love the person I promised to cherish. If I leave the marriage, I know I will be shadowed by guilt. I fear it will never let me go free.

B: You feel like the characters in Jean Paul Sartre's play *No Exit*. Three people died and went to Hell. They were welcomed by a guide who ushered them down a long hallway into a pleasant room, appointed with comfortable chairs, refreshments, and soft music in the background. They thought, "Maybe Hell isn't so bad after all." Their guide told them to make themselves comfortable and disappeared out the door.

The three guests began to talk. The better acquainted

they became, the more they disliked each other. Finally, one man could stand it no longer. He knew he had to get out of there and started for the door. It was then that he discovered that the door was sealed. No Exit. No way out. Then he knew he was in Hell—"the state of existence where you are trapped in painful relationships."[1]

P: That is the way I feel.

B: The people in *No Exit* had used up their options, but I like Victor Frankl's thinking on options. He spoke of the last option—"the freedom to choose our attitude toward our fate."[2]

P: What did Frankl mean?

B: I think Frankl was speaking of "boundary" situations—experiences like a radical loss that cannot be regained, or a great sin which cannot be undone, or being told that you have a terminal illness. When you know you are dying there remains the option of choosing your attitude toward your fate. Kubler-Ross's clinical research on dying persons revealed that people die well if they reach a stage called "acceptance." Acceptance is the choice of an attitude toward fate and in that choice the human spirit triumphs over the illness. Acceptance comes when we are ready to die, when we have completed unfinished business and have set our spiritual house in order.

Divorce is a boundary experience, especially for a person of evangelical persuasion. As we have discussed

---

1. Jean-Paul Sartre, *"No Exit" and Three Other Plays* (New York: Vintage Press, 1956).

2. Victor Frankl, *Man's Search for Meaning* (New York: Pocket Books, 1963).

so many times, your beliefs tell you to stay in your marriage, but your beliefs also tell you to cherish your husband. You say you cannot find it within yourself to cherish him nor can you give yourself permission to leave him. No exit.

P: My Christian friends tell me that I am to "love *and* cherish" Pierce. They say I must love as well as cherish him. Then they add, "Love is not a sentiment; it is a behavior." They argue persuasively that love in marriage may be jump-started by romance but that it runs on commitment and caring. They are not able to tell me whether people should marry when they are not romantically in love. Some say "no" and some say "yes," if you are both Christians, well matched and are committed to treating each other as Christians. But when I press them, asking each if they were romantically in love when they married, virtually all of them say "yes." Occasionally, someone will hedge the question by saying, "I don't know—how can you know if you are in love when you are hardly old enough to get your driver's license?" In short, I don't think my Christian friends—the ones preaching to me that romantic love is not the basis for marriage—were standing in line to get into loveless marriages.

Those who are willing to concede my point retort, "Yes, we marry for love and romance but romance fades and unless responsible, mutually need filling, giving and taking behaviors are in place, romance won't carry the marriage." Sounds plausible, especially to someone as easily persuaded as I.

B: So your friends seem to think responsibility is more important than romance. I'm reminded of Lois Wyse's poem, *A Cozy Heart*.

Once I thought that love
Was tempestuous,
Tumultuous,

'Kiss me quick.'

I was wrong.

Love is usually a very comfortable way of life,
A cozy heart,
Kisses on the cheek,
'Wear your rubbers and blow your nose.'

And what keeps a love so cozy?
The fact that every so often love is
(Kiss me quick.)[3]

Wyse seems to think that compatibility and romance are *both* essential ingredients in marriage. I'm reminded that the Song of Songs *and* 1 Corinthians are *both* in the Bible.

P: What do you mean?

B: The song celebrates love as romance. "Let him kiss me with the kisses of his mouth—for your love is more delightful than wine." "Take me away with you—let us hurry." "If you find my lover, tell him I am faint with love." "Turn your eyes from me; they overwhelm me."

And so on—eight chapters in praise of romantic love, redolent with the sensory language and tactile detail characteristic of men and women head over mattress in love! Furthermore, their language is typical

---

3. Lois Wyse, *Love Poems for the Very Married* (New York: World Publishing Company, 1967).

of the Hebraic attitude toward the human body. It was Gnostic Greeks who hated the body and wanted to get rid of it. Hebrews reveled in the sensory delight of the body. They saw flesh as a gift of God and sexuality as a special sign of His goodness. They didn't however, have much use for promiscuity, free love, or adultery!

First Corinthians, chapter thirteen, is in no way prudish or ascetic. The fifteenth chapter also clearly rejects Greek notions of a split between body and soul or of the superiority of the spiritual over the physical. However, 1 Corinthians 13, the celebrated "love chapter," describes love as a behavior rather than a sentiment. Love is *agape*, a caring, self-giving, committed mindset which finds its motivation and model in the servant lifestyle of Jesus. The chapter has no words against romantic, sentimental love, but it celebrates love in the form of ethical and caring treatment of others rather than the romantic mix of sex, narcissism, and fantasy so characteristic of contemporary "lovers." So: "Love is patient, love is kind. It does not envy, it does not boast, it is not proud. It is not rude, it is not self-seeking, it is not easily angered, it keeps no record of wrongs. Love does not delight in evil but rejoices with the truth. It always protects, always trusts, always hopes, always perseveres. Love never fails."

An idealistic description of love, to be sure. It is an accurate picture of the love of Jesus and it is clear Paul believed that Christians are empowered to love after the manner of Jesus, but the married partner has not yet been found whose love "never fails."

We do fail. We do fail . . . and we will fail again. If married persons could live out 1 Corinthians 13 there would be fewer failures. If every person entering marriage would take a vow to live by 1 Corinthians 13, I mean a serious vow, not merely something repeated after the minister, the divorce rate must drop.

P: I don't want to fail in my marriage. What can I do to keep from failing?

B: Do you think you have done all you can to keep from failing?

P: I believe I have, but my marriage remains an empty shell and I have no feeling of attachment to Pierce.

B: My prayers are with you.

P: Thanks.

5

There Is Therefore Now No Condemnation

About eight months later, Peg called to tell me that she was filing for divorce. She said she was firm in her decision. A year passed without my hearing from Peg, but now she was in my office again. I had hoped to see a happier face, a peaceful countenance under that dark hair, but the marks of tension were still evident.

P: The divorce is final and I feel awful.

B: You did make the decision, but feel it was the wrong one?

P: No, it was the right decision. I couldn't get my heart into the marriage. I tried. Pierce deserved better even though he wanted to keep us together. I also felt the children needed a parental model of two people loving each other, rather than an unbalanced, one-sided relationship. It was the hardest decision I ever made, but it was my decision.

B: I respect your courage and I have a feel for the struggle. But you still feel awful?

P: I can't escape the feeling that I have deliberately,

intentionally, and willfully broken God's command for marriage.

B: I see.

P: I hear certain Scriptures quoted in adult classes at church or from the pulpit that hit me like God's hammer.

B: (Now I was beginning to shift uneasily in my chair. There was something about the drift of her narrative which stirred anxiety in me.) Do you remember the particular Scripture which fell on you like a hammer?

P: I can't quote chapter and verse, but I remember the gist. "Whoever knows what is right to do, but doesn't do it, has committed sin."

B: Yes, that is in James 4:17.

P: In another place, Jesus said that sin against the Holy Spirit will not be forgiven.

B: You had it almost right. (I picked up the New Testament and read from Matt. 12:30-32.) "Jesus said, 'He who is not with me is against me, and he who does not gather with me scatters. And so I tell you, every sin and blasphemy will be forgiven men, but the blasphemy against the Spirit will not be forgiven. Anyone who speaks a word against the Son of Man will be forgiven, either in this age or in the age to come.'"

The text does not say that God will not forgive the divorced; it says He will not forgive blasphemers.

P: What is a blasphemer?

B: According to the context of this passage, a blasphemer is a person who attributes the good work of Christ to demons. I take it to mean one who rejects Christ completely. It is a clear choice between good and evil rather than the ambiguous choice between two good options or two relatively but not absolutely bad options.

P: You lost me somewhere.

B: I'm sorry. (My convoluted way of speaking often leaves me talking to myself, while my audience steals quietly away.)

When you divorced, you made a choice between two options, neither of which was good. Both options were mixed, good and bad. It was good to stay with Pierce, but bad not to love him. God ordains marriage, but He also ordains a loving relationship in marriage. He said, "The two shall become one." If you divorce, you violate His words, "What God has joined together let not man put asunder." You seemed to be in a position where you violate one or the other command.

P: Of one thing I am convinced. I did everything in my power to love Pierce and I gave it plenty of time. I don't think that is a rationalization; I have a clear conscience on that.

B: I know. I've listened to your struggle for a long time now.

P: I've had drummed into my head all my life that divorce is sinful. It's like an old tape playing in the back of my mind. It makes me sad and guilty.

B: I understand. But I did not say that divorce is not sinful. I think a sinless divorce is rare. I do not possess the knowledge which tells me which is and which isn't, but most divorce must be sinful.

P: What? Now you've flipped me again. I thought you said that divorce is sometimes a good decision!

B: I did. But just because it is a good decision doesn't mean it isn't sinful. I believe that nothing we do is free from sin. After all, we are sinners, so everything we touch is marked with the imprint of our nature. I also believe that we are seldom faced with a choice between pure good and pure evil. Our decisions are more likely to agonize between lesser and greater evil or lesser and greater good than between absolute evil and absolute good.

P: Well, I know if I had stayed with Pierce that I couldn't fulfill the good of loving him. If I left him I couldn't fulfill the good of keeping the marriage together. But I still feel terrible. I can't forgive myself.

B: You have been divorced for a year but you still blame yourself as the one who wanted out of the marriage.

P: I have stopped going to church because it makes me feel guilty.

B: Peg, what I'm hearing sounds like heavy self-judgment. It is a good thing to take responsibility for our actions but it is a real trap to get caught up in the "Herr Turbicide" syndrome.

P: What do you mean by the Herr Turbicide syndrome?

B: I refer to Martin Luther's personal work with a Moravian named John Schlaginhauffen. Luther affectionately nicknamed him "Herr Turbicide." I will call him "H.T." for short. H.T. was like the man who said to Jesus, "I believe; help my unbelief." You have something in common with H.T., Peg, because you share his difficulty in believing God has forgiven you. It is a problem most Christians feel at certain times. Luther himself, the great proclaimer of forgiveness of sin, formulated in the doctrine of justification by faith, suffered from doubt that his sins were, in fact, forgiven. For this reason he could identify with H.T. In attempting to remove the hair shirt from H.T., Luther, no doubt, was lifting it from himself. Peg, I am going to loan you this book by H.G. Haile, *Luther, An Experiment in Biography*,[1] because you have a lot in common with H.T. But let me read you a little now from the book. "When Luther would discover the morose H.T. in one of his pensive spells, he would say, 'A penny for your thoughts', or 'What are you sitting there pondering? Be joyful in the Lord!'

" 'Ah, dear Herr Doctor, I would truly like to, but many frightening trials prevent me.'

" 'What kind of trials?'

" 'Ah, I really cannot express how I feel.' "

But Martin Luther would not be put off. He laid out a scholarly analysis of all possible doubts which a Christian might have. His own greatest trial, he said, had to do with faith in the Holy Spirit, for he sometimes doubted his own calling. H.T. resisted Luther's attempts to disabuse him of his doubts with the refrain, "When I think about God, it comes into my mind: 'Thou art a sinner! God will not hear you. He is angry with you.' "

But Luther snorted, "If I am not to pray until I become devout, when shall I pray? If Satan recites to you, 'Now we know that God heareth not sinners,' you must turn it right around and say, 'I pray because I am a sinner.' "

Luther turned sardonic: "Oh, we are happy if we can have peace of mind. But we want it on our own terms, not as a gift from God." (Peg, if you could understand the implications of that one line, you could be delivered of your self-blame. "Our own terms" refers to the heresy

---

1. H.G. Haile, *Luther, An Experiment in Biography* (Garden City, NY: Doubleday, 1980).

of works-righteousness. This heresy believes salvation turns on what *we* do, not on what God has done. It is the belief that your acceptance by God is based on your action—whether *you* did the right thing, whether you made the right decision, whether you are culpable or not. Thus, your deeds accuse or excuse you. In that framework, the mercy of God is irrelevant, because human action makes you or breaks you. Luther's point is penetrating—in the works-righteousness mindset, acceptance as a gift cannot be tolerated because it is incompatible with the deep and fixed conviction that acceptance is always earned. Luther was quick to see that such a mindset kept H.T. out of the kingdom, that kingdom of grace where there is no damnation.)

Luther would often remind H.T. of the words in 2 Corinthians 12:7-10, "My grace is sufficient for you . . . my strength is perfected in weakness." Then H.T. would ask, "Herr Doctor, are you saying it behooves me to remain a scoundrel and a sinner?"

In his best sardonic manner, Luther would quote from Psalm 51: "That thou mightest be justified when thou speakest and be clear when thou judgest." Then the dear Doctor might reel off some of his "devil advice": "When the devil comes at night to worry me, this is what I say to him: 'Devil, I have to sleep now. That is God's commandment, for us to work by day and sleep by night.' If he keeps on nagging me and trots out my sins, then I answer: 'Sweet devil, I know the whole list.' " Luther seemed to operate on the theory that the devil could not stand a sense of humor, especially the self-deprecating kind. *Maybe the devil is the devil precisely because he takes himself more seriously than anyone else in all the universe.*

Luther continued: "If he won't cease to accuse me of my sins, I say in contempt: 'Sancte Sathana, ora pro me. Oh, you never did anything wrong. Thou art alone blest. Go now to God and find grace for yourself. If you want to perform your good offices on me, then I will say, "Physician, heal thyself." ' "

Luther's biographer, Haile, asks, "Would it be proper to explain Luther's 'Satan' as a kind of metaphor for self-reproach . . . ?" Call it what you will, it was no metaphor for Luther. Luther focused on the biblical language describing Satan in the role of accuser. Luther believed that the grace of God was the only sure defense against the accuser. Justification by faith in the grace of Jesus Christ was Luther's "mighty fortress."

> By our own strength is nothing won.
> We court at once disaster.
> There fights for us the champion
> Whom God has named our Master.
> Would you know His name
> Jesus Christ the same.
> The field is his to hold it.

Martin Luther was past fifty when he came to know John Schlaginhauffen. No doubt, "Herr Turbicide" reminded old Doctor Luther of young Luther, the monk, standing before his father confessor, Johann von Staupitz, with the same heavy conscience and dreadful fear of God's wrath. The great Luther scholar, Roland Bainton, tells us that "The content of the (Luther's) depression was always the same, the loss of faith that God is good and that he is good to me."[2]

---

2. Roland H. Bainton, *Here I Stand, A Life of Martin Luther* (New York: Abingdon, A Mentor Book, 1950), p. 282.

Peg, that's your problem, and very often it's my problem as well—*the loss of faith that God is good.* When Luther would lose this faith, Staupitz would point Luther away from himself, away from subjective self-blaming, to the objective work of Jesus Christ on the cross, which is offered as a sheer gift. Staupitz reminded Luther of Psalm 32:1,2: "Blessed is he whose transgression is forgiven, whose sin is covered. Blessed is the man to whom the Lord imputes no iniquity."

Later, when Luther was lecturing on the Psalms, he noticed that Paul quoted this passage from Psalm 32 in Romans 4. The liberating insight which broke in on Luther was that righteousness is a gift rather than an achievement. He saw verses in Romans which said, "Abraham believed God, and it was credited to him as righteousness," and "God credits righteousness apart from works," and "the promise comes by faith, so that it may be by grace," and "the words, 'it was credited to him' were written not for him alone, but also for us, to whom God will credit righteousness—for us who believe in him who raised Jesus our Lord from the dead. He was delivered over to death for our sins and was raised to life for our justification. Therefore, since we have been justified through faith, we have peace with God through our Lord Jesus Christ, through whom we have gained access by faith into this grace in which we now stand."

The word "credited" (from *logizomai,* to count) means the believer in Christ is placed in a position where her sins are not counted against her while the righteousness of Christ is counted for her, so that God sees the righteousness and purity of Christ rather than our sins.

Luther's reflection on the first five chapters of Romans brought him to understand the paradox that the "justice" or "righteousness" of God was a perfection that God demanded of all mankind but freely gave to those who approached Christ in faith. This understanding freed Martin Luther from an oppressive conscience. He said, "This straightway made me feel as though reborn and as though I had entered through open gates into Paradise itself."[3]

Luther would add, "God does a strange work in order to perform a work that is properly his own." This strange work is, "first to destroy and to turn to nothing whatever is in us before he gives us his own."

"Peg, I believe God is doing that strange work in you. He is showing you that there is no way to get peace about your divorce until you cease self-blame and begin to live in God's mercy. I leave you with this verse. Memorize it and repeat it to yourself as needed: 'There is therefore now no condemnation for those who are in Christ Jesus'" (Rom. 8:1).

That was the last time I saw Peg. I would like to believe that her disappearance from my appointment book means that she finally discovered Martin Luther's secret of relief from an oppressive conscience. I do not know. I do know there is no other way.

As Luther said,

It was for this He came down from heaven, where He dwelt in the righteous, that He might also dwell in sinners. Think about this love of His and you will see how beautifully it will comfort and sustain you. For if

---

3. Martin Luther, *Lectures on Romans*, The Library of Christian Classics, Volume XV (Philadelphia: Westminster Press, 1961), p. 37.

it is only by our own efforts and striving that we can achieve a quiet conscience, what did He die for? You will therefore find peace only in Him, in faith despairing in yourself and your own works, and thus you will learn that as He took you up and made your sins His own, He made His righteousness yours.[4]

---

4. Ibid., p. 48.

6

The Deepest Pain In The Dilemma:
What Will Happen to the Children?

In a seminar for divorced persons, I asked the participants to state the most difficult challenges they faced. Here are their responses:

"I had to do a lot of relearning of what it is like not to have someone with whom to share frustrations."

"How do you learn to like yourself?"

"I've learned to change my priorities. It is more important to spend time with the kids than to keep the house neat."

"It is hard to keep my identity as a man and as a father and still fill in the gaps for their mother who is not here."

"It hurts that my son does not have a male model."

"Dating causes friction with my children."

"I no longer have a scapegoat for my problems!"

Five of the seven responses relate to concern for the children. Divorcing parents are more anxious about their children than any other stress brought on by divorce. The anxiety is well founded. A sixth grade child described his feelings about his parents' divorce in this way: "It feels like you are dying inside all the time. It feels like someone you love a lot has died."

The pain the extended family feels, the anxiety that grandparents, aunts and uncles feel, arises from concern for the little ones. Post-divorce conflict between parents is usually over the children. The question is often asked: is it better for parents to remain in a bad marriage for the sake of the children or to divorce? It is a tough question. But if you were to put the question to the children, they would say, "stay together," unless there is something really scary about the behavior of their parents. The reasons for divorcing that parents give their children are not usually persuasive to the children. "We don't love each other anymore." ("Then maybe you'll stop loving me?"). "Your mother and father feel it would be better for us to live apart." ("Why?"). Parents are well advised to be prepared to give a decent answer to that question; most are not.

The divorce rate more than doubled in the United States in the decade of the seventies. Since then, thankfully, it has leveled off, but the various divorce statistics record the highly negative impact of divorce on children.

In Sedgwick County, Kansas, where I once lived, four hundred divorces are being filed each month, one-half of them involving children.

In child custody cases, fifty percent will come back to the court for changes, which means that parents continue to fight over children after the divorce.

In the fifth year after divorce, seventy to eighty percent of non-custodial parents are not paying support.

Since mothers are most likely to have custody, this situation has created what has been called "the feminization of poverty."

Thirty-five percent of children in Wichita, Kansas, public schools live in single parent homes. Fifty percent of public school children in Wichita have experienced their parents' separation or divorce.[1]

The impact on children includes the following dynamics:

Shock: Linda Franke, in her book *Growing Up Divorced*,[2] estimates that 8% of the children of divorce have no warning at all. She quotes Hugh McIsaac, Director of the Conciliation Court in Los Angeles: "A child is better prepared by his parents for a tonsillectomy or appendectomy than he is for divorce. He wakes up one morning and one very significant person in his life has moved out. You can't imagine how destructive that is for a child."[3]

Why don't kids see the divorce coming? Probably because parents try to conceal the critical nature of their problems from the children as long as possible. In addition, the children ward off bad news through denial.

When parents do finally tell the children that a divorce will occur, they frequently give the children vague explanations. Inadequate interpretations of the causes of the divorce deepen the child's sense of injustice. She sees herself as a victim of a great hurt which makes no sense.

---

1. Statistics from the Domestic Court, Sedgwick County, Wichita, KS.
2. Linda Franke, *Growing Up Divorced* (New York: Simon and Schuster, 1983).
3. Ibid.

Psychiatrist Richard Gardiner contends that children should be told plainly why the parents are divorcing. He suggests telling the kids flat-out: "Your father drinks too much and since he won't get help, I refuse to tolerate it any longer," or, "Your mother spends so much money that we are constantly in debt." When such statements are true, children can accept a divorce much better than they can accept one based on global explanations. Gardiner adds, "Real people have flaws as well as admirable qualities. The parent who won't tell is depriving the child of useful information!"[4] No doubt there are exceptions to Gardiner's counsel, just as there are exceptions to all generalizations. Nevertheless, a plausible interpretation to children of the reasons for a divorce reduces the shock of the dissolution.

Grief: The origin of the term "stepchild" is traced to the old English word for grieving, "steop." The word is appropriate, for a stepchild is usually grieving the loss or threatened loss of the non-custodial parent. The child may also be grieving the loss of the custodial parent to the stepparent. That is, the child may feel the stepparent has replaced the child in the parent's affection. At the very least, the child is forced to share the parent with the stepparent and may experience this sharing as loss. Thus, children of divorce experience a "series" of losses: at divorce, the loss of the non-custodial parent and the loss of the nuclear family; at the remarriage of the custodial parent the loss of that parent to the stepparent; at the remarriage of the non-custodial parent, the loss of that parent to his or her new spouse. In addition, divorce often forces a move to a different house, neigh-

---

4. Richard Gardiner, quoted in Franke, *op. cit.*

borhood, and school. Familiar surroundings and friends may be lost. Thus, the children of divorce experience "grief upon grief." Their parents also are passing through multiple loss and readjustment. Pervasive grief is the inevitable pain in families split by divorce.

Moreover, it is difficult to come to closure on this kind of grief. Where is the grave for a dead marriage? How do you grieve for people who go out of your life only to return periodically? You grieve over and over again, and you find it difficult to achieve a decent distance from your grief.

Children may show the symptoms of their grief in one or more of the following ways:

Decline in the quality of school work
Fighting with siblings or classmates
Apathy and withdrawal
Drug addiction
Promiscuity
Living dangerously, taking risks, becoming accident prone
Rebelliousness
Anger—older children may manifest the worst displays of anger. The reason why older children tend to show more anger to divorced parents than young children is obscure. My best guess: older children may feel their own difficult behavior in childhood strained the parental marriage and they are now projecting that guilt onto the parents.
Psychosomatic illnesses
Encopresis and enuresis in younger children
Virtually any of the entire range of behavioral problems of children may appear in children of divorce.

Guilt: Small children frequently feel they have "caused the divorce," especially when their parents fought a lot over the children. The fight may have been triggered by differences over how the child should be disciplined. The logic of the child seems to go something like this: "The fight was about me; that made them angry with each other; the anger split them; therefore, I caused the divorce." Divorcing parents do well to take responsibility for the divorce and to make clear to the children that they are not the ones responsible for the parental problems. A rebellious child may have strained the marriage, but divorce is a parental decision.

The child who is forced to take sides with one parent may feel she has abandoned the other. Such a scenario creates confusion for the child at best and guilt at worst.

Reconciliation fantasies: Young children in particular dream that their parents will reconcile. The child may become de facto marital therapist, seeking to heal the broken marriage. Pre-adolescent and adolescent children may be quite shrewd and active in attempts to sabotage the next marriage of the custodial parent. Such malignancy is based on the fantasy that if the marriage is broken up the natural parents will reunite. The child may achieve the purpose of undermining the second marriage. Disillusionment will quickly follow, for seldom will the custodial parent return to the first spouse (it is interesting to note that the biblical record explicitly forbids a return to a first marriage after an intervening marriage—Deuteronomy 24:1-4).

Adjusting to the unique experience of living in a "blended" family: Since about eighty percent of divorced parents under age thirty-five will remarry, large numbers of children are living in stepfamilies or blended families. It is estimated that at least one out of six children live in such families in the United States![5] My sense is that this statistic is low.

1. A number of thorny issues may arise in stepfamilies. A child who has been living alone with a divorced mother will usually become strongly bonded to that mother. Mother is also very attached to the child. When mom begins to date, the child will experience fear of separation from mom, and a strong resentment to mom's suitor. The mother's sensitivity to the slightest nuance of emotional change in the child may make it difficult for her to develop a bonding to the new man in her life. In turn, the man may be annoyed by mom's undue preoccupation with her child. If marriage follows, the child may make excessive demands on mom's time and attention. Unless mom is firm with the child and unless she can handle the guilt of turning some of her attention away from the child, her new relationship may come under severe strain.

2. Children may feel supplanted by the stepparent. The teenage daughter who had become de facto "mother" of the house and the teenage boy who had become the acting "man" of the house, feel the threat of being pushed out of their roles by the stepparent. The new stepparent will need to be very sensitive to these older children and would be well advised to avoid power struggles with them.

---

5. Emily B. and John S. Visher, *Stepfamilies* (New York: Bruner/Mazel, 1979).

3. How well children do in a reconstituted or blended family may depend on the parent's understanding of the following "givens" in step-families:

   a. A blended family is not as cohesive as a nuclear family. Parents/stepparents in a reconstituted family usually assume that "being family" means a close-knit group where stepparents are to relate to stepchildren like "natural" parents. That assumption is the reef on which the good ship "stepfamily" goes aground. A stepfamily is a much looser organized family just because the relationships are not usually as close between family members who do not share a biological connection. If a stepfamily, especially the adults, can drop the illusion that the family can be The Brady Bunch, they will have made the first giant stride toward stabilization. Beliefs shape behavior and false beliefs sabotage relationships. The belief that a stepfamily can be like a nuclear family is understandable but unrealistic.

   b. The role of a stepparent is determined in large measure by the ages of the stepchildren. If the stepchildren are quite young, not older than six, the stepparent has a chance of becoming de facto parent to the child. Stepparent and young stepchild are in a position to become bonded to each other, especially if the non-custodial biological parent has faded out of the child's life. If the stepchild is older, the stepparent will be well advised to define himself as friend rather than parent to the child. The stepparent should refer discipline needs for older children to the biological parent. Discipline will not be "accepted" by the child (acceptance is defined as the child's feeling that the stepparent has a "right" to discipline the child) until a good relationship is established between them. Older children will seldom ever "accept" discipline from a stepparent. Unless this reality is accepted by the stepparent, trouble is brewing.

c. The primary task for stepparents is to give priority to the nurturance of their marital relationship. Stepchildren will distract couples in many ways, but, paradoxically, the couple will help their children most by putting the marriage first. Neglect of the children is not the counsel here. The counsel is that the children tend to nag and pull at the adults so hard that unless the couple tends to the marriage, the family may disintegrate. The children feel most secure when they see a solid relationship between the adults. When this priority is maintained, the family has a better chance to jell.

Divorce is always hard for everyone, but here are some tips which may make it a little less traumatic:

1. Prepare the children in advance of the divorce.
2. Tell the children the truth, except when the truth accomplishes nothing except additional hurt. Never lie to children, but some things are best left unsaid.
3. Let the children know the divorce is final. There will be no return to the previous marriage.
4. Where possible, help the child feel good about the non-custodial parent.
5. The child has a need to respect both parents.

6. A child's self-respect diminishes with diminished respect of either parent.
7. During a divorce and its aftermath, children need extra attention and love from parents.
8. The child may believe that if parents stop loving each other they may stop loving the children; that child needs reassurance of parental love.
9. Do not use your child as a weapon of anger directed at your former spouse.
10. After a divorce, parents tend to feel a child's misbehavior was caused by the divorce. It may have been, indeed, but the parent must not allow guilt to sidetrack appropriate discipline.
11. You can survive a divorce and remarriage, but you can survive it much better if you study the dynamics of stepfamilies. The following books are recommended:

    Miller, Arlyn. *Guidelines for Divorcing Parents (Helping Children Through the Trauma of Divorce)*, Family Life Publication, Inc. Box 427, Saluda, NC, 28773, 1979.

    Sinberg, Janet. *Divorce Is a Grown-Up Problem*, Avon Books, The Hearst Corp., New York, NY, 1978. This book is illustrated for very young children.

    Visher, John and Emily, *Stepfamilies*, Citadel Press, Secaucas, NJ, 1979. The best available on stepparenting.

    Westberg, Granger, *Good Grief*, Fortress Press, Philadelphia, 1971. A classic on grief and loss.
12. Divorce always hurts children but sometimes staying married hurts them even more. The biblical guideline here is, "God has called us to live in peace" (1 Cor. 7:15). Divorce hurts children less if

parents are able to arrange a reasonably amicable and businesslike relationship after divorce. Ongoing parental fighting upsets children more than the divorce itself. I believe most children can adjust to their parents' divorce if mom and pop can bury the hatchet. If not, the hatchet will cut and maim every family member and may even become an instrument for digging graves.

The answer to the question, "Should we stay married for the children's sake?" must be "yes, if you can conduct your marriage in a way that does not damage your children." If not, divorce is a solution only if parents can be at peace after the divorce. Since life is not plastic, readily molding itself to our desire, the search for peace, whether married or divorced, is quite elusive. Nevertheless, we adults must continue to search, for the children first, and for ourselves as well.

13. The two most important tips for divorcing parents concerned about the well-being of their children are: (a) children need to continue a good relationship with the non-custodial or non-residential parent wherever possible. (b) If parents have post-divorce conflict, they should exclude the children from the disagreements whenever possible. Seldom is this done. Most divorced persons continue their personal struggle through the children. Children become message runners for people who can't resolve their issues face to face. Children become pawns on the chessboard where parents seek to checkmate each other.

Community resources can be mobilized to provide

social, legal, and therapeutic structures for enhancing cleaner and saner divorces. One of the most innovative programs is the brainchild of Domestic Court Judge James Beasley of Wichita, Kansas. All divorcing couples with minor children are required to take a two session course at the Wichita Guidance Center called "Children of Divorce." The workshop offers practical guidelines to help parents understand and deal with children's reactions to divorce. The workshop emphasizes that families, especially children, can successfully adjust to divorce. Recognizing children's stress symptoms, distinguishing between appropriate and inappropriate behaviors, examining visitation from the child's perspective, and maintaining parental roles while dissolving marital roles are just a few of the issues this workshop addresses. Using a positive, educational approach, the Children of Divorce program seeks to diffuse the impact of divorce on the family.[6]

Judge Beasley believes that "the most important decision made at the Court House is about families." The guideline he follows for judicial decision making is, "What is in the children's best interests?" He holds that "the wave of the future is back to the way it used to be—where it takes the entire community to raise a child."[7]

That last statement is especially meaningful because it reveals awareness that community agencies have provided few resources for divorcing families—that families often were forced to go it alone, to flounder in

---

6. Lecture from Judge James Beasley, Domestic Court, Sedgwick County, Wichita, KS.
7. Ibid.

their isolation. But now programs like Judge Beasley's are "coming alongside" families passing through divorce. When divorce becomes a necessity, enlightened and compassionate community resources can make the rough passage a little smoother for parents and their children.

Most American communities of size have numerous agencies assisting families through divorce, including mediation services. Referrals can be obtained from Domestic Courts and Mental Health agencies.

7

Lingering Questions About Peg

When I think of Peg, nagging doubts remain—doubts about myself. Did I cover all the bases? Did I act as a Christian? Was I faithful to my identity as a Christian theologian? Was that identity overshadowed by my dual identity as a marriage and family therapist? Was the Bible my authority or did the theories of "behavioral science" subtly mold my responses to Peg's dilemma?

I also have questions about Peg. Who was Peg, really? I know that my appraisal of her is not infallible. And what criteria should I use to evaluate her—biblical truth or psychology? Or both? I name my stance—God's word is the first and last word. I am willing to learn from any source, but Jesus Christ is the Way, the Truth, and the Life. He is to be trusted above any other source of information. When I talked with Peg, was I faithful to that belief? My readers can judge while I search my own heart.

Another question: Was Peg a product of the culture

of narcissism? Am I a product of that culture? In his classic work, *Habits of the Heart,* sociologist Robert Bellah traces how American society has developed into a culture which believes in happiness of the self, by the self, and for the self. Self-autonomy, self-happiness, and self-fulfillment have been made into an idol. Bellah believes this idolatry threatens the tissue which holds us together. We are like the Geizenslaw Brothers. "Split the blanket down the middle; that's all you can do when love goes wrong." Was Peg a Geizenslaw?

The elevation of the American divorce rate to fifty percent occurred from the sixties onward, in that era when the self was being celebrated at fever pitch. The literature of pop psychology is replete with the idolatry of self: "How to Pull Your Own Strings," "The Joy of Feeling Good," and many others.

Bellah believes that the modern elevation of the self can be traced in large measure, to the influence of the psychotherapeutic professions. I agree with Bellah's words in the following statement:

> While the culture of manager and therapist does not speak in the language of traditional moralities, it nonetheless proffers a normative order of life, with character ideals, images of the good life, and methods of attaining it. *Yet it is an understanding of life generally hostile to older ideas of moral order* [emphasis mine]. Its center is the autonomous individual, presumed able to choose the roles he will play and commitments he will make, not on the basis of higher truths but according to the criterion of life effectiveness as the individual judges it.[1]

---

1. Robert Bellah, *Habits of the Heart* (Berkeley, CA: University of California Press, 1985), p. 47.

Was Peg acting out of the culture of the autonomous self, the narcissistic "therapeutic" culture, rather than the way of agape love, which is self-denying rather than self-seeking? Was the proper appraisal of Peg not that she loved Pierce too little but that she loved herself too much?

Any Christian contemplating divorce must face this question. Christians in "pseudo" marriages must especially face it. On every critical decision, the Christian must search his/her soul, asking the hard question, is self the engine driving my decision? Christian therapists must hold the client and themselves to this soul-searching.

When I review the hours I spent with Peg, I am not sure I was sufficiently thorough in exploring the extent to which Peg may have been held in thrall to the culture of narcissism. "O for a wonderful place called 'The Land of Beginning Again!'" Alas:

The moving finger writes; and, having writ,
Moves on: nor all thy piety nor wit
Shall lure it back to cancel half a line,
Nor all thy tears wash out a word of it.
—Fitzgerald, "Rubaiyat of Omar Khayyam."

The phrase, "The culture of narcissism," derives from the Greek myth of the handsome Narcissus. He loved himself unto death. Emil Brunner said, "God accepts man's emancipation from Himself; He burdens him with it."[2]

When Walt Whitman declared, "I celebrate myself,

---

2. Emil Brunner, *Man in Revolt* (Philadelphia: Westminster, 1939), p. 134.

and sing myself," he thought he was announcing the emancipation of the self; instead he announced the bondage of the self to itself, the awful burden of self-love. Bonhoeffer said that "Jesus bids us come and die." It is the self which must die, the narcissistic self, the self dying from an overdose of love curved back on itself.

Peg may, indeed, have been both the victim and the perpetrator of the culture of narcissism. The culture gives us a line of vision which can only see reflections rather than reality. Everything which is seen reflects the self. Wherever the self looks it sees itself because the conceptual lens is pre-focused.

Robert Coles writes that, "for psychology, the self is the only or main form of reality."[3]

Psychology has dominated the consciousness of Western Civilization in the last half of the twentieth century. The burden of the emancipated self began to be felt in the middle to late sixties, when vast numbers of people began to loosen their commitments—because self needs were elevated above social needs. The burdensome products are the "Baby-busters" and "Generation X," persons with an overriding consumer orientation, persons who sit loose to commitments, persons who pass in and out of relationships, churches, and jobs like nomads looking for the next oasis, like sailors without a port. Christians also drink deeply from the fountain of this culture, not knowing it is poisoned, unaware of its alien source. Counter-awareness and insight come from drinking deeply at the fountain of Scripture, the only lens which accurately

---

3. Robert Coles, "Civility and Psychology," *Daedalus*, Summer, 1980, p. 137.

reflects the self. That lens focuses on such passages as Gal. 2:20, "I have been crucified with Christ and I no longer live, but Christ lives in me. The life I live in the body, I live by faith in the Son of God, who loved me and gave himself for me."

Only the crucified self has a right to leave a marriage and then only when greater harm would be done by remaining. And who can know which would do greater harm? Only the person who is a crucified self and only the person who prays, whether that person is the client or the therapist.

We must face the hard truth that not even the crucified self or the praying self can *always* know whether to stay or leave. But if we pray out of a crucified self, we are more likely to act wisely. Those who act in haste will repent at leisure. Never take a step without prayer. Sometimes steps must be taken, decisions must be made, even when absolute certainty eludes us.

Finally, when divorce is over and done, the mercy of God is the only solvent for the stains of guilt.

Part Two:

AVOIDING THE TRAP

8

Preventing Divorce in the Church

Kenneth Chafin, in a fine little article entitled "When a Marriage Fails," said that a close friend confided that his daughter had been through a divorce and he didn't know how to treat her. Chafin responded with a question: "If her husband had died, what would you do?" The friend immediately began to describe helpful responses to a grieving person. When he finished, Chafin reminded him, "Your son-in-law didn't die, but the marriage did. This death is in some ways more painful. Treat it that way and you'll know what to do."[1]

Chafin's point is well taken. Freshly divorced persons, especially those who resisted divorce, are grieving the death of the marriage. They are also grieving having been rejected.

The first rule of pastoral care to the grieving is to make contact. Persons who have suffered a loss should be contacted as soon as possible. Caring persons,

---

1. Kenneth Chafin, *Guideposts*, April, 1980.

whether ministers, friends, or family, will take initiative in making contact with the grieving. The contact may come before, during, or after the loss. Contact will usually be made at all those times, but contact must be made close in time to the actual loss. The contact is made in the form of warm, human, and tangible *presence*. The paraclete, the Holy Spirit, is "alongside us" in the form of a caring human presence. When grieving is acute, presence is more important than words. I remember none of the sermon at my father's funeral, but I will never forget the friends who hugged me. Ministers come alongside people when they have lost a loved one, but less frequently do they stand alongside when people are divorcing. Thus, the divorced are further isolated and sometimes left alone to fend for themselves.

Divorced persons are avoided, we often say, because we do not know what to say to them. Actually, we avoid the grieving to avoid our own anxiety. We don't need to say anything, but we do need to make a caring contact. We tend to avoid the person whom we assumed to be chiefly responsible for the divorce, but that person may need our care as well. Some churches have "disfellowshipped," or "churched," or "shunned," or "excommunicated," the person thought responsible for the divorce. The New Testament has no record of persons disfellowshipped for divorce. Even when church discipline was done for other reasons, it was a form of pastoral care, so that the person's "spirit might be saved on the day of the Lord" (1 Cor. 5:5). Contemporary discipline is more likely to be a form of punishment. It requires great insight and self-honesty to avoid projecting our anxiety and insecurity about our own marriages on to another's marital crisis. If church discipline is needed, it is not pastoral care unless the Christian community or its representatives are willing to become involved, hearing all sides, listening to the complexity of the marital dilemmas, feeling the pain of the real situation, offering concern out of a deep sense that "all have sinned and have come short of the glory of God." Pastoral care from a safe emotional distance is not pastoral and is not care. Pastoral care is not sentimental, but neither is it superficial. Pastoral care givers also have decisions to make, and sometimes the choice is between "coming alongside" or "passing by on the other side."

It is often difficult to know why marriages fail. We are prone to slick and easy explanations of why John and Mary divorced. The less we know about John and Mary's marriage, the easier it is to make assumptions. Marriage is inherently difficult, and the real wonder is a marriage that succeeds. But even when the cause of marital breakdown seems evident, someone needs to give care to the person who is responsible for the demise of the marriage, as well as to the person who is the victim (one must be wary of easy generalizations about responsibility and victimization). Pastoral care which comes in the form of confrontation may embody genuine caring and is certainly to be preferred to avoidance of those divorcing or divorced.

Preventive Pastoral Care

When people have already divorced, pastoral care comes after the fact. But the preferred form of pastoral care is to come alongside people when marital problems arise rather than when they have reached crisis proportions. Unfortunately, the opportunity to provide such care is less frequent because people hide their marital problems from others or from themselves until they reach a crisis point. Ministers and marriage and family therapists seldom have the luxury of working with a marriage before it reaches the crisis stage.

Nevertheless, I believe that churches can provide "pre-crisis" pastoral care of marriages through the church's regular education program and through marriage enrichment programs. Marriage preparation can be taught in the context of the church's regular Christian Education program. Persons as young as high school juniors could be enrolled in short term courses which are taught by persons with knowledge of marriage and family interaction patterns.

The time to do premarital counseling is before persons are engaged to be married. Research on "cognitive dissonance" has shown that typical premarital counseling is not effective in preventing serious marital problems. "Cognitive dissonance" is the phenomenon of not being able to hear unpleasant information because of an emotional resistance to the data presented. Couples typically receive premarital counseling after they have become engaged. At that point in their relationship, they don't want doubts raised or to be told that they need to make changes or confront significant relationship issues. The rosy glow of romantic love closes their eyes to relational realism. If such couples could be brought into "pre-engagement" counseling rather than "premarital" counseling, the counseling might be more effective. Couples who learn before they are engaged that they are not suited to each other are much more likely to stop the march toward marriage than couples who are engaged. The church needs to start a revolution in premarital counseling by preparing couples to do their counseling before engagement. The premarital test called "Prepare"[2] claims 80-90% accuracy in predicting divorce. The claim is based on research. If churches could get pre-engaged couples to take "Prepare," they might do significant work to anticipate and prevent divorce.

Couples who are committed to the Christian faith are more likely to stay married than those who are not serious Christians. Research on couples who are members of the Christian Reformed Church revealed that the divorce rate among these couples was about five percent, as compared to about forty percent (at the time of research, 1981) for the general population in the United States.[3] Follow-up research on these Christian couples revealed that they struggle with typical marital problems, but that they seldom see divorce as a solution to those problems. In light of this research, it follows that the best referral for people with marital problems is for *the church to make a referral to itself.* My meaning is this: the above quoted research suggests that if the church carefully teaches the Christian faith to its young and faithfully teaches the implications of that faith to those approaching marriageable age but not yet engaged, this teaching will help persons to build enduring marital relationships. Let the church refer its young to the church's native resources for marriage. Let the referral be made before marital crisis appears, even before engagements are made. To make such referrals,

---

2. David H. Olson and Blaine J. Flowers, "Predicting Marital Success with Prepare: A Predictive Validity Study," *Journal of Marital and Family Therapy*, October, 1986.

3. Henry Holstege and Larry Teitsma, "Four Christian Reformed Congregations: Marital and Family Strengths" (*The Banner*, December 14, 1981).

the church will need to do innovative work on its educational program. Every church should have pre-engagement classes for its young and attendance should be virtually mandatory. It's time for the church to stop wringing its hands about divorce and begin to put those hands to work building foundations for marriage.

Pastoral Care Through Referrals

Nevertheless, ministers and friends or associates of couples in marital crisis will be confronted with the necessity of making referrals to professional marital therapists. These professionals are usually identified by their membership in the American Association for Marriage and Family Therapy. Such membership does not guarantee competency, but it certainly makes it more likely. It is always preferable to make referrals to persons we know and trust, but when we do not know a therapist, she is more likely to be trustworthy if she possesses the appropriate clinical credentials.

I believe most ministers should regularly make referrals after one to three interviews, because most ministers do not possess the skills to deal with the complexities of marital crisis, and they certainly do not have the time. One of the first acts of a minister new to a congregation should be to find competent referral sources in or near his community and to begin to develop a relationship with the preferred referral persons.

Referring ministers or other persons making referrals can use the following checklist as a guide for the referral process:

1. Have your referral source ready in advance. Know the professional personally.

2. Have the professional's telephone number available, but let the referred person make the call. The willingness to call for an appointment is a measure of the willingness to work on the problem.

3. The referral is not likely to be successful for purposes of reconciliation if one spouse clearly wants out of the marriage. The referral can be made, but don't be disappointed with the marital therapist if he/she does not work a miracle.

   Most ministers, especially evangelical ministers, have their own "cognitive dissonance" with spouses wanting out of a marriage. The minister does not want to hear that, and may reject the person who has the courage to honestly state his/her feeling that the marriage is over. Neither does the minister want to hear the marriage counselor's assessment that the marriage is over. Such a minister may fire that referral source and hire a new one, one who is more inclined to believe in miracles. Unfortunately, the miracle that changes the mind of the person bent on divorce seldom occurs.

4. More typically, a minister is faced by a spouse who is ambivalent or confused about the marriage. Commitment may be shaky, but when some investment in the marriage remains, that bonding should be nurtured by the minister's encouragement to the couple to work on their problems and by the minister's continuing support while the couple is in counseling. Referral is not abandonment. The marital therapist is on the firing line but the minister stays on the supply line. The therapist also needs the minister's moral support, and each needs the other's consultation.

5. Not infrequently, the referral issue has to do with what I call a "flip-flop." A flip-flop occurs when a spouse previously uninterested in his spouse's attempts to improve the marriage, becomes strongly motivated to correct the marital conflict after the spouse separates or files for divorce. A typical scenario is a spouse who has been irresponsible for years, suddenly coming to repentance and making promises to change after his spouse leaves him or threatens to leave. The promises may or may not be kept; time alone will tell. When they are sincere, they will not usually be convincing unless supported by positive and constructive behavioral change. "By their fruits you shall know them."

In such a case, the pastoral strategy is to encourage the separating spouse to put decisions to divorce on hold until time reveals whether the prodigal's verbalizations of repentance have substance. The pastoral strategy for the contrite spouse is to encourage personal growth. If such persons have a drinking problem or drug problem, a referral to AA or to a substance abuse center is imperative, together with a simultaneous referral for marital therapy. Such treatment may be costly, but it is less expensive than divorce.

While the contrite spouse who has come late to repentance is making responsible changes, work may need to be done in therapy with a view to assist the "straight" spouse in exploring how they may have contributed to the drinking problem or other destructive behavior of their spouse. Enabling behavior in a straight spouse is a common phenomenon in these marriages. Competent marital therapists will address such critical issues. Most ministers will not be aware of these complex, but decisive marital dynamics.

Churches can make their referrals much more convincing and effective if they establish a financial aid fund for persons needing counseling, or if they financially support a church-related counseling center. The salvation of one marriage will repay the funds invested in such a service, for the break-up of the marriage is a financial loss to the church as well as to the couple. Granted, financial considerations are not the incentive for such referrals; nonetheless, Jesus taught that prudence is not beneath those who would build the Kingdom (Luke 16:1-9). Jesus is usually presented as an idealist, but His realism is quite striking.

6. A minister may have also to deal with a counselee's resistance to a referral. He will be more successful if he knows the referral source and has confidence in that person. Although people go to counselors in droves in this country, there is a first time for everyone and most are quite apprehensive about it. They may need encouragement and reassurance from the referring person.

A minister should be aware that some dependent persons may resist a referral by stating that they are not willing to see anyone else but the minister. Such a stance is manipulative and the minister should decline without guilt to do further counseling. To do so, he will have to come to terms with his own rescue needs. Ministers are vulnerable to such manipulation because of the inherent caring in a minister's heart and because of the church's long tradition as a caring community.

A minister often represents and embodies that tradition. But the terms of care offered cannot be dictated by the recipients of the help. Perceived need is not necessarily real need.

7. Not only must the referring person protect the confidence of the persons he refers, he must also protect the reputation of the person to whom he refers. Chafin remarks:

"A friend said to me, 'I'm not going to send anyone else to that counselor. I sent a couple and they still got a divorce.' My reply was, 'Yes, and a lot of people die in the emergency room of the hospital not because of inadequate care but because of the shape they were in when they got there.' "[4]

A person referred may come back saying they did not like the counselor or what he/she did. Ministers have been known to take such reports at face value. Integrity calls for a check on the accuracy of such reports by a telephone call to the therapist. The therapist may have a different point of view on what transpired in the counseling office. Therapists make mistakes, and anyone can have a bad day, but therapists are vulnerable to referring persons who are gullible. Therapists are defenseless against distorted reports of their work. When the referring person does not check the disgruntled report directly with the therapist, the referring person is unethical.

If a minister does check with the therapist and finds

---

4. Chafin, *Guideposts*.

there is another and different side to the story, he is faced with the pastoral responsibility of a confrontational interview with the person(s) he had sought to refer. The minister's authority and discipline may be called for and, if so, he will need to approach that stage of pastoral care with the support and solidarity of his fellow elders. A minister's family counseling is confidential, but he has ethical freedom and responsibility to consult with the elders on critical issues. It is not a breach of pastoral ethics to do so, especially when pastoral counseling and referral evolve into an issue of confrontation and discipline. The minister may be well advised, however, to routinely obtain written releases for consultation with elders or other professionals. If such releases are not forthcoming, the minister should decline to continue counseling. The culture is growing more litigious and ministers face growing vulnerability.

Realized Forgiveness for the Divorced Person

When divorce has become a reality, the pastoral care goal is to help the divorced to experience what James Emerson calls "realized forgiveness."[5] Emerson defines realized forgiveness as "the awareness of forgiveness to such a degree that a person is free from the guilt he feels."[6] (The work with Peg described in chapter six was an attempt to bring her into realized forgiveness.)

Forgiveness is not therapeutic until a person is released from guilt. Forgiveness is objectively real the moment a person asks for God's mercy, but forgiveness

---

5. James G. Emerson, Jr., *Divorce, the Church and Remarriage* (Philadelphia: Westminster Press, 1961).
6. Ibid., p. 23.

·is not subjectively real until that mercy is appropriated. The goal of pastoral care with divorced persons is to help them realize that both objective and subjective forgiveness are possible. It is a lofty goal, but fully promised in the New Testament (Rom. 8:1). The process toward realized forgiveness may include the following issues:

1. Helping a divorced person acknowledge and accept responsibility for behavior which did in fact contribute to the demise of the marriage. Few persons emerge from divorce with halos intact. The church's historic tendency to be preoccupied with "grounds" for divorce, makes the church vulnerable to the assumption that the guilty and the innocent can be readily identified. It might be wise for the church to start with the assumption that "all have sinned and come short of the glory of God."

2. Helping divorced persons manifesting guilt to avoid the blind alley of "self-forgiveness." Divorced Christians may be heard to say, "I know God forgives me, but I cannot forgive myself."

    A minister/Bible teacher can be very helpful to such a person by biblical instruction which makes plain that self-forgiveness is a distinctly non-biblical and anti-Christian concept (Ex. 20:3; Mark 2:7; 1 Cor. 4:3, 4). Self-forgiveness should be relabeled for what it is: idolatry. The person who says, "I know that God forgives me, but I cannot forgive myself" is manifestly idolatrous. They have set themselves above the word of God. Their own conscience is given higher authority than Scripture. Such persons may feel as they do because they have not experienced forgiveness from the church.

Nevertheless, they must still face the question of whether they will continue to elevate self above God. If God forgives but the self does not, then the self believes in itself more than it believes in God. Relief will come when such a person repents, not only of the marital sins, but also of the sin of idolatry. Only ministers or biblically informed counselors are prepared to deal with this problem.

3. Offering biblical "absolution." The Protestant reaction to the medieval abuse of the church's ministry of mediation healing, has left non-Catholics without a doctrine of absolution. Absolution is a powerful resource for pastoral care to guilt-laden persons. The risen Christ "breathed" on His disciples and said, "Receive the Holy Spirit. If you forgive anyone his sins, they are forgiven; if you do not forgive them, they are not forgiven" (John 20:22-23). I take these words of Christ to mean that the church is given authority to offer reassurance that persons who hear the grace of God and repent of their sins are in fact forgiven. The concrete form of this ministry of reassurance is found in James 5:13-16:

"Is any one of you in trouble? He should pray. Is anyone happy? Let him sing songs of praise. Is any one of you sick? He should call the elders of the church to pray over him and anoint him with oil in the name of the Lord. And the prayer offered in faith will make the sick person well; the Lord will raise him up. If he has sinned, he will be forgiven. Therefore confess your sins to each other and pray for each other so that you may be healed. The prayer of a righteous man is powerful and effective."

The ministry of healing described here was led by elders. No apostles are mentioned. Thus, elders did carry on a ministry of healing in the early church. This fact suggests that the words of Jesus in John 20:22-23 describe a work of absolution which is not limited to the apostles, but given to the whole church and mediated through the church's representative leaders. I define "absolution" as the reassurance of the forgiveness of sins to repentant persons on the basis of the proclamation of the gospel of grace both in word and symbol.[7] Protestants and other evangelical Christian groups have relied heavily on the word but lightly upon symbols. In the James 5 passage, the symbols which mediate absolution include the physical presence of the elders and anointing with oil. It is likely that elders "laid hands" on the ill person, for such was a common practice in the New Testament church.

The process followed in James 5 included mutual confession of sins. I take it that this is a reminder that both elders and those for whom they pray are sinners before God, human, vulnerable, flawed, and daily in need of grace. Yet these flawed persons have the gospel in "earthen vessels" and they mediate this gospel in their prayers and presence. The anointing with oil points beyond the

---

7. Paul Pruyser, "The Master Hand," in *The New Shape of Pastoral Theology* (Nashville: Abingdon Press, 1969).

flawed persons to the authority of the Holy Spirit to say, "Your sins are forgiven."

The guilt laden person may confess the specific sins which caused the guilt and may receive absolution in the assurance, "if he has committed sins, they will be forgiven him." This powerful healing ministry has been neglected in non-Catholic and non-charismatic churches. It is a gift to the whole church. The ministry of the gift requires no special credentials except faith and obedience to the teachings of John 20:22-23 and James 5:13-16.

4. Helping divorced persons move toward the goal of personal reconciliation even though marital reconciliation is not possible. We are still required to forgive, even though we cannot reconcile. The church sometimes assumes that reconciliation and forgiveness are synonymous. Whenever we forgive, we should also reconcile, where possible. We are always to forgive, even when unreconciled.

Scripture stresses the ideal of forgiveness and reconciliation, but Scripture is realistic. Scripture does not sanctify divorce, but it does sanction it. It sanctions it in those cases where it is necessary. It sanctions divorce as a concession to human limitations. Although Scripture recognized that some persons can no longer live together, it does not accept the refusal of those persons to forgive each other.

God may give us time to forgive, but He will not give us the freedom not to forgive. I define forgiveness of the ex-spouse as willingness to pray for the former spouse, willingness to have God heal bitterness, and willingness to turn that person over to God, since God alone is their judge. I think the prayer should continue until the person is ready to surrender bitterness, and then I think the prayer should be discontinued. I think the prayer should be stopped because the goal now is to move the ex-spouse out of one's consciousness as much as possible. Commit them to the care of God and then get on with life. Prolonged prayer for an ex-spouse may keep one in bondage to the memories and hurts from the first marriage. Focus now on the new life derived from God's grace and accept the teaching that those who "put their hand to the plow," must not look back (Luke 9:62).

9

Justification by Faith:
Ground Zero for the Divorcing/Divorced and for the Church

Attitudes of Christians toward divorce are intertwined with beliefs about the nature of the church. Theologies of the church and theologies of divorce cannot be separated. What we think about divorce and how we feel about the divorced flow out of what we think about the church. We will complete the sentence, "the divorced are _____ ," on the basis of how we complete the sentence, "the church is _____ ."

The nature and structure of ministry to the divorcing or divorced will also be shaped by the church's self-perception. The question: "What do we do?" is preceded by the question: "Who are we?" If church ministers and elders are asked, "What is the nature of the church?", their answers will provide hints about their attitudes toward divorce. If we know what the church believes about itself, we can predict how the church will respond when one of its members is divorced.

What the church believes about itself can be probed

by the use of two fundamental questions: Is the church a congregation of the well or a community of the wounded? Is the church an inclusive or exclusive community?

In his book *The Wounded Healer*, Henri Nouwen relates an old legend from the Talmud:

> Rabbi Yoshua ben Levi came upon Elijah the prophet while he was standing at the entrance of Rabbi Simeon ben Yohai's cave . . .
> He asked Elijah, "When will the Messiah come?"
> Elijah replied, "Go and ask Him yourself."
> "Where is he?"
> "Sitting at the gates of the city."
> "How shall I know Him?"
> "He is sitting among the poor covered with wounds. The others unbind their wounds at the same time and then bind them up again. But He unbinds one at a time and binds it up again, saying to Himself, 'Perhaps I shall be needed: If so I must be ready so as not to delay for a moment.'"[1]

The Messiah sits among the wounded. He Himself is wounded. The Talmudic legend is consistent with the way Jesus defined Himself and His church. He said, "It is not the healthy who need a doctor, but the sick. But go and learn what this means: 'I desire mercy, not sacrifice.' For I have not come to call the righteous, but sinners" (Matt. 9:12, 13).

Jesus said the members of the church are those who acknowledge their unworthiness and who know that they are members by the mercy of God. Those who are

---

1. Henry Nouwen, *The Wounded Healer* (New York: Image Books, 1990).

confident of their own righteousness are excluded.

> To some who were confident of their own righteous-
> ness and looked down on everybody else, Jesus told
> this parable:
> "Two men went up to the temple to pray, one a
> Pharisee and the other a tax collector. The Pharisee
> stood up and prayed about himself: 'God, I thank you
> that I am not like the other men—robbers, evildoers,
> adulterers—or even like this tax collector. I fast twice a
> week and give a tenth of all I get.' But the tax collector
> stood at a distance. He would not even look up to
> heaven, but beat his breast and said, 'God, have mercy
> on me, a sinner.' I tell you that this man, rather than
> the other, went home justified before God. For every-
> one who exalts himself will be humbled, and he who
> humbles himself will be exalted" (Luke 18:9-14).

The members of the church are self-conscious
sinners, defined as those who are aware of their human-
ness, their vulnerability, their capacity for pride, for
inordinate self-love, their inclination to insist on their
own way (1 Cor. 13:5, RSV), their tendency to forget that
they have nothing they did not first receive, their
proclivity for forgetting that they entered the church by
the grace of God and remain in the church by that same
grace. The Christian is a "justified" sinner, but nevertheless a sinner (1 John 1:18). He/she cannot make the
Pharisaic claim, "I am not like other men." We are like
all other men in that we share their human nature. The
not-divorced are also like the divorced in that they share
the same human nature and they also could become
divorced. Those of us who have never been divorced
should be cautious about congratulating ourselves as if a
stable marriage were our own achievement.

Jesus uses the word "justified" for the first time in His parable of the Pharisee and the tax collector. The root of the word is *dikaios*, "righteous," or "one who is such as he ought to be." Thayer's Greek lexicon gives four facets of the meaning of *dikaios*: "1. Virtuous, keeping the commands of God; 2. Innocent, guiltless; 3. Preeminently, of him whose way of thinking, feeling, and acting is wholly conformed to the will of God, and who therefore needs no rectification in heart or life. (In this sense Christ alone can be called *dikaios*.) 4. Approved of God, acceptable to God."

By these definitions, especially points two and three, there are no righteous. Paul's teachings support this assertion, when he flatly states: "There is none righteous, no not one," and, "All have sinned and fallen short of the glory of God" (Rom. 3:10, 23). Even the virtuous fall short of the glory of God, for God is absolutely virtuous.

In his parable of the Pharisee and the tax collector, Jesus gives righteousness an absolutely new meaning. The "righteous" are those who know themselves to be unrighteous and who throw themselves on the mercy of God. The unrighteous are those who are "confident of their own righteousness" and who look down on others. The "justified" or "righteous" are those whose plea, "God, have mercy on me, a sinner," has been heard. The righteous are the forgiven. The righteous are the recipients of mercy. The righteous are those who humble themselves. Such persons are "exalted" or lifted up to the high level of joy known only to those who say, "By the grace of God I am what I am" (1 Cor. 15:10).

By this definition, there *are* righteous people, but they are the people who have *received* righteousness rather than those who *achieved* it, because righteousness is a gift.

Paul's epistle to the Romans develops the theme of righteousness and defines it as a gift. Righteousness is revealed "in the gospel," that is, in what Christ has done for us in His death and resurrection. Since what Christ has done for us is a sheer gift, it can only be received by faith, that is by receptivity, by openness and trust, by belief and obedience. Obedience in baptism, for example, is an act of believing; trust that God will do what He said He would do when we are baptized, namely forgive our sins and give us the Holy Spirit. Forgiveness of sins and the gift of the Spirit are not achieved by being baptized but *received* when we are baptized (Acts 2:38, 22:16). The believing, repentant, trusting, and obedient person is placed "in Christ" when baptized (Gal. 3:26-27) and such a person is considered by God to be righteous, not because they are without sin but because they are "in Christ." "For our sake he made him to be sin who knew no sin, so that in him we might become the righteousness of God" (2 Cor. 5:21, RSV).

Those who are in Christ are treated by God as if they had no sin. The "as if" is the meaning of "justification." Jesus introduced the word "justified" in His parable of the Pharisee and the tax collector. Paul draws out the meaning of justification in Romans under the concept of justification as a legal term. After stating that "all have sinned and fall short of the glory of God," Paul announces that we "are justified freely by his grace through the redemption that came by Christ Jesus" (Rom. 3:23-24). Paul's word for "justified" has the same root (*dikaios*) as the word for righteousness. "Justified" is a legal term. The justified person is a person who has been called into court, has been declared guilty, but who has nevertheless received a pardon.

In Romans, chapter four, Paul introduces an additional word to describe the justified person. This is the word *logizomai,* translated in the NIV as "credited." *Logizomai* is an accounting word, meaning "to count" or "compute." Paul says that Abraham's faith was "counted" as righteousness (Rom. 4:4, 5). He declares that David's faith meant that his sins would not be "counted" against him (Rom. 4:6-8). This righteousness is "credited" "apart from works" (Rom. 4:6). In Romans 4:22-5:2, the conclusion is made that those who have faith in Christ will have the righteousness of Christ credited to their account, while their own unrighteousness is not counted against them. Such persons stand justified. "We have gained access by faith into this grace in which we now stand" (Rom. 5:2). *The members of the church are the justified, persons who can never claim any righteousness for themselves. Such standing is not disqualified by divorce, nor is it gained by being non-divorced.* The Messiah sits among the wounded. The church is a community of the wounded. The church is the congregation of the justified, the recipients of mercy, the celebrants of grace.

The answer to the second question, is the church an exclusive or inclusive community, is implicit in the foregoing discussion of justification by faith. The exclusiveness of the church can only be defined as those who base their identity "exclusively" on the doctrine of justification by faith. Such has not always been the case, however, in the history of the church. The epistles to the Galatians and Romans were written primarily against those who based church membership on merit, virtue, and law keeping, rather than on the grace of God. Paul is emphatic: "We . . . know that a man is not justified by observing the law, but by faith in Jesus Christ. So we, too, have put our faith in Christ Jesus that we may be justified by faith in Christ and not by observing the law, because by observing the law no one will be justified" (Gal. 2:15-16). Again: "You who are trying to be justified by law have been alienated from Christ; you have fallen away from grace" (Gal. 5:4).

In his book, *Christ and Culture*,[2] H. Richard Niebuhr outlines the various attitudes the church has taken toward secular society. He summarized these attitudes under the headings of Christ Against Culture, The Christ of Culture, Christ Above Culture, Christ and Culture in Paradox and Christ the Transformer of Culture. If we substitute the word "church" for "Christ" in Niebuhr's language, his meaning is clarified. Yet, Niebuhr's language is justified, for he wants to emphasize that the church takes its attitude toward culture from its belief about how its Lord stands in relation to culture.

The "Christ Against Culture" stance finds the church rejecting and opposing culture. In this stance the key word is "withdrawal." The text for this position is "Come out from among them and be separate." By this definition, the members of the church are the most dedicated and holy rather than the strugglers and searchers.

The "Christ of Culture" stance finds the church accommodating itself to culture or even taking its lead

---

2. H. Richard Niebuhr, *Christ and Culture* (New York: Harper and Row, 1951).

from culture. Such a stance can be either "liberal" or "conservative," depending on which culture the church seeks to honor. For example, the Ku Klux Klan is an accommodation of the church to a conservative culture, while the philosophy of Teilhard de Chardin is an accommodation of Christianity to Darwinian evolution. The American Pastoral Counseling movement, in its earlier stages, made a thoroughgoing accommodation of the Christian faith to Freud and to the "client centered" psychotherapeutic theories of Carl Rogers. The key word in this stance is "accommodation."

The "Christ Above Culture" stance finds the church integrating the Christian faith with culture. This stance seeks to draw the best from both worlds and to show how they illuminate and support each other. From this point of view, various facets of culture may be considered morally neutral but open to be utilized as a "carrier" of the Christian message. For example, the tunes and instruments of secular music are sometimes given Christian lyrics. In this stance, the key words are "integration" and "utilization."

The "Christ and Culture in Paradox" stance finds the church in an uneasy tension with culture. The church is aware that its presuppositions are in clash with culture at various points, but also aware that God can do His work through Pharaoh. This means that the church is open to the possibility that it can learn from "secular" culture. Thus, in this view, the church is willing to carry on a dialogue with non-Christians in all branches of human learning, in science and the humanities, even with those who hold assumptions radically opposite to Christian presuppositions. The key word in this stance is "dialogue." But genuine dialogue is not possible where each party is unaware of its assumptions while insensitive to and uninformed about the assumptions of the fellow dialogist. In short, in dialogue you have to know what you believe and what the other party believes and to be able to *hear* as well as to *speak*. In the history of Christian culture, Thomas Aquinas stands as one of the great dialogists.

The "Christ the Transformer of Culture" stance finds the church seeking to convert the total culture so that culture and Christianity become co-extensive. Alexander Campbell preached the doctrine of Christ the transformer of culture in his millennial theology. He believed that the realization of Christian unity on the basis of the restoration of the primitive New Testament church would result in the conversion of the world to Christ and thus usher in a thousand years of peace. The journal in which he propagated this and other views was named the *Millennial Harbinger*. All "primitivist" views (those movements which advocate a return to first century or primitive Christianity) seek to transform culture by a return to biblical norms.

On those occasions in history when the church and culture have become virtually co-extensive, as in the Middle Ages, the church has ended by accommodating itself to culture. The culture whose ruler is also its spiritual head has frequently resorted to religious persecution, the worst form of tyranny just because the authority claimed for it is God Himself. Awareness of this historical fact is largely the reason why Thomas Jefferson and the other founding fathers of American democracy established the doctrine of separation of church and state. In any case, the key word in the "Christ, the Transformer of Culture" stance is "conversion."

What does Niebuhr's discussion of "Christ and Culture" have to do with the issue of divorce? It calls Christians to reflect on their own most basic assumptions about the church. It confronts Christians with the question: Do I believe in an inclusive or exclusive church? If you can answer that question you will know why you hold a given attitude toward the divorced.

Niebuhr's discussion can help us clarify our views on divorce, in part because he invites us to ask: which of the five views is closest to a biblical doctrine of the church vis-à-vis culture? Niebuhr is not contending that any of these views is the biblical perspective; he holds that the church has adopted one or more of these views at various points in its history.

Scripture could be quoted to support at least four of the five viewpoints set forth in Niebuhr's discussion. I do not believe the accommodation view set forth in the Christ of Culture stance can find Scriptural support. Nor do I feel the issue can be settled by quoting isolated Scriptures which appear to support or deny Niebuhr's schematic.

The more productive questions for the church are: which view is most consistent with the gospel? Which view is consistent with justification by faith? Which view flows out of the person of Christ, who He was, what He did, what He taught? These questions cannot be addressed by quoting bits and scraps of the New Testament. They are addressed when they are set alongside the basic theme of the New Testament. That theme is the gospel of the grace of God in the Person of a Savior who said, "Whoever comes to me, I will never drive away" (John 6:37).

I hold to an inclusive view of the church because I

think that view is most consistent with the basic meaning of the gospel. The inclusive view means that the church is for sinners and strugglers, for the hurt and broken, for the searchers and questioners, for the grieving and dying, in short, for us. The biblical doctrines of sin and righteousness establish that even persons who have always been "good," even persons whose moral profile is impeccable, fall short of the glory of God. They may never have been hurt or broken, never struggled, never searched and questioned (their number must be few), but their goodness is relative rather than absolute and they possess the same kind of human body, mind, and soul as do the divorced. The church is called to throw its net around the fortunate and unfortunate, the well and the wounded. The church is a sanctuary, a refuge for "all who are weary and heavy laden," as well as for those who are unscarred and upbeat.

It is true that the church is to be "in the world, but not of the world." It is true that the church is called to preach repentance as well as forgiveness. But the preaching of repentance is an act of grace because it is "the goodness of God which leads us to repentance" (Rom. 2:4).

It is true that the church is called to a ministry of discipline. It is to confront those who are unforgiving (Matt. 18:15-35) while remembering that a good shepherd will "leave the ninety-nine on the hills and go to look for the one that wandered off" (Matt. 18:12). The church is to withdraw fellowship from the incestuous, the greedy, the idolater, the slanderer, the drunkard, and swindler (1 Cor. 5:1-11). "With such a man do not even eat." The divorced are not in this list; the "sexually immoral" are. Some divorced persons are sexually immoral, but many are not.

Withdrawal of fellowship is not the withdrawal of love and care. It is the act of holding persons responsible for their behavior, of penetrating their denial, of calling them to reform while providing support for that reform. It is not abandonment or avoidance. It is the withdrawal of all support for the unacceptable behavior.

 The inclusive church is not the sentimental church, nor does it practice cheap grace. The inclusive church is grounded in grace, so much so that we care enough to confront church members who are practicing self-destructive and relationship-destructive behavior. The call to repentance is a gracious call because it tries to free persons from self-destructive behavior.

 The church is a community filled with the Holy Spirit. The Spirit convicts the world of "sin, righteousness, and judgment" (John 16:8-11). He is the Comforter, who comforts us by calling us to repentance that we may be saved from self-destructive acts. He is also "the Spirit of truth" (John 15:26). Since the Spirit of truth resides in the Christian community, surely the church  can tell the difference between a struggler and the unrepentant, between the brokenhearted and the smug, between those who are seeking to find God's will for their lives and those who have closed their hearts to grace. We are told, "if any of you lacks wisdom, he should ask God, who gives generously to all without finding fault" (James 1:5) (A grace filled, Spirit-filled church will find the wisdom to know when to be inclusive and when to be exclusive) Nevertheless, I believe the church's basic stance toward the divorced should be inclusive, here defined as grace in God's people, for

God's people, by the gospel, and for our healing. The wounded Messiah still sits among the wounded.

In his book, *Pastoral Care in Social Problems*,[3] Wayne Oates outlines various positions the church has taken on divorce. He calls them "laissez-faire," "forensic," and "confrontational/therapeutic." Each position corresponds to a particular view of the church.

The laissez-faire position avoids serious involvement with divorced persons. On the one extreme you have the "marrying parson" who will marry anyone who comes down the pike as long as they have a marriage license and an honorarium. The Little Brown Church near Nashua, Iowa is a shrine for the practice of an uninvolved ministry of marriage. On the other extreme is the legalist who "does not extend any type of ministry to the divorced, apart from telling them he does not marry divorced persons."[4] Such legalism provides a safe castle protecting its occupants from any serious involvement with the complexities, ambiguities, and anxieties experienced by the divorcing and divorced.

The forensic position is a more moderate form of legalism. Protestants are forensic when they ask questions like, were these persons Christians when they divorced? In this view, if the answer is "no," remarriage is permissible. Implied in the question is the view that Christians who have been divorced cannot be forgiven, while non-Christians may since "all their past sins were forgiven when they became Christians." The upshot of

---

3. Wayne Oates, *Pastoral Care and Social Problems* (Grand Rapids: Baker Book House, 1975).
4. Ibid.

such a position is that Christians can't use the doctrine of forgiveness of sins when they really need it, while it is readily available to non-Christians.

Catholic theology is forensic in its doctrine of annulment, which does not allow divorce but is able to declare that there was never a marriage. The upshot of such a doctrine is that each child implicitly if not explicitly is considered to be illegitimate. Forensic views are legalistic views moved up to a slightly higher level of sophistry. They are more interested in the rules than they are in people.

The confrontational/therapeutic stance is very close to the concept of the inclusive church. According to Oates, in this stance a ministry to the divorcing and divorced will: 1. Attempt to establish a good relationship between the church and the couple in question. 2. Utilize treatment resources in the community by referrals. 3. Follow up on these referrals. 4. Take people where they are and try to help them grow in grace and integrity.

Oates comments:

> The reflective pastor does not marry couples apart from their durable and responsible commitment to the Christian faith. Whether they have been divorced is secondary to this.[5]

With this value in mind, Oates makes the following practical suggestions for church policy on questions of divorce and remarriage:[6]

1. Ministers and elders should share decision

---

5. Ibid.
6. Ibid.

making about divorce situations. To leave such decisions to a minister is a laissez-faire attitude on the part
of church leaders. Ministry in crucial situations requires
consultation, a team approach, mutual supportiveness,
and the wisdom derived from shared prayer and
thought. Ministers should not allow elders to abandon
them to a solitary ministry to the divorcing/divorced.

2. The church as a matter of policy should require
advance notice for any marriage. This policy will help
the church avoid a casual approach to the ministry to
marriage.

3. The church should expect and enable their ministers to deal with difficult family conflict situations, either
with competent personal counseling or competent referrals. I would add that if the church is serious about this
it will be willing to pay the fees for the minister's training and supervision in marriage and family dynamics,
and will also establish a fund to help couples pay fees to
the professional to whom they may be referred. Or the
church may establish its own professional counseling
staff. Smaller churches may join with other congregations in the support of an area church counseling center.
The church will be willing to do this unless its concern
for families is merely verbalized rather than actualized.

4. The church should instruct, expect, and even
require its members to present their family conflicts to
some person or persons within the fellowship of believers before going to courts of law. In other words, the
church should take initiative to encourage couples to
exhaust all resources for a Christian solution to their
problems before they use the courts. The church will
encourage their members to seek this counsel from
trusted and competent Christians before they use legal

resources. Persons with serious marriage problems should seek out a Christian who is also professionally competent in marriage and family therapy. Serious marital conflict is too complex to be handled well by lay persons, no matter how devout they may be. Christians do not have the possibility of an ethical divorce unless they have exhausted all sources of reconciliation, with the highest priority given to the counsel of trusted, competent, and grace filled persons in the Christian community.

Epilogue
A Deeper Root on the Windward Side

On the social Richter scale, divorce is 8.5. Its epicenter is the divorcing couple but the shock waves shake the children, the extended family, the friends, the church, and threaten to rip the entire fabric of society. Sensitive and thoughtful people, of whatever religious or ethical persuasion, cannot, as a general principle, pronounce divorce "good." Nevertheless, in biblical history at least from the time of Moses, divorce was a fact of life which had to be acknowledged and regulated. Divorce will ever be present in a fallen world, but divorced people can be healed, can regain a sense of wholeness, can recover from hurt and bitterness, can experience the peace of God, and can live in the church with joy and without shame. Whether they do, in fact, recover from the shock of divorce, depends in large measure on whether they find a church which is a community of grace.

In the entire history of Christendom, no one has presented a theology of divorce and remarriage which all Christians could accept. This book has presented a theology of divorce and remarriage which is grounded in the theology of grace, the doctrine which I believe is the central theme of Scripture. I do not expect that everyone who reads this volume will accept its point of view, but I do hope that divorced persons may find healing in these pages. I also hope that those who work with the divorcing or divorced may be able to use this book.

The kind of ministry the church offers to divorcing or divorced people will always be connected to and shaped by the church's *theology* of divorce. It is impossible for the church to talk about pastoral care to the divorced as if it were exclusively a pragmatic concern. What Christians do (pragmatic), with, to, or for persons whose marriages are breaking or have broken, flows directly out of theology, that is, how we interpret the biblical materials on divorce, together with the controlling theological theme in which ministry is grounded. Standing behind each position on divorce is a theological theme such as grace or legalism. Standing behind all theologies of divorce is a concept of God. What we feel about divorced people is determined by what we believe about God. What we believe about God is shaped by Scripture, but our view of Scripture is filtered through our parents and grandparents, our Sunday School teachers, our ministers, and our personal experiences. There is no such thing as a presuppositionless theology. (The foregoing statement is, of course, a presupposition!) Yet, we *can* read Scripture in an honest attempt to reexamine our assumptions.

My own theology of divorce, indeed my entire theology, was once heavily legalistic. I am sad to confess that as a young minister I declined to officiate at the wedding of my own sister for no other reason than the fact her chosen was divorced. I shudder now at my own self-righteousness. Only the thought of God's mercy gives me any peace. My present theology of divorce, indeed my entire theology, is based in the doctrine of grace. How I moved from one to the other is a part of the mystery of God's providence. The theology of my youth and the theology of my gray years were both shaped by my concept of God. The former god was a celestial policeman who never failed to catch the guilty. The latter god is like Jesus. That God is grace. This is my controlling theological theme. It is more than a theological theme. It is an existential reality. It is personal. It is also liberating. It has been for me the path to freedom. It alone has made the Christian life possible. It alone has made the church a center of joyous life. It alone has made it possible to live with myself, and whether others know it or not, made it possible for them to live with me. When those anguished moments come when people cannot live together, grace will help us weave new patterns from broken threads.

I do not know the author of the following poem, but the poet sums up my final word to the divorced.

> Defeat may serve as well as victory
> To shake the soul and let the glory out.
> When the great oak is straining in the wind,
> The boughs drink in a new beauty, and the trunk
> Sends down a deeper root on the windward side.
> Only the soul that knows the mighty grief,
> Can know the mighty rapture.
> Sorrows come to stretch our spaces
> In the heart for joy.

Selected Bibliography

Bainton, Roland H. *Here I Stand, A Life of Martin Luther*. New York: Abingdon Press, A Mentor Book, 1950.

Bellah, Robert. *Habits of the Heart*. Berkeley: University of California Press, 1985.

Brunner, Emil. *Man in Revolt*. Philadelphia: Westminster, 1939.

Chafin, Kenneth. "When A Marriage Fails." *Guideposts*. April, 1980.

Coles, Robert. "Civility and Psychology." *Daedalus*. Summer, 1980.

Cruden, Alexander. *Cruden's Complete Concordance*. Philadelphia: C. Winston Company, 1949.

Emerson, James G., Jr. *Divorce, the Church and Remarriage*. Philadelphia: Westminster Press, 1961.

Franke, Linda. *Growing Up Divorced*. New York: Simon and Schuster, 1983.

Frankl, Victor. *Man's Search for Meaning*. New York: Pocket Books, 1963.

Haile, H.G. *Luther, An Experiment in Biography*. Garden City, NY: Doubleday, 1980.

Hicks, Olan. *What the Bible Says About Marriage, Divorce, and Remarriage*. Joplin, MO: College Press Publishing, 1987.

Holstege, Henry and Larry Teitsma. "Four Christian Reformed Congregations: Marital and Family Strengths." *The Banner*, December 14, 1981.

Luther, Martin. *Lectures on Romans*. The Library of Christian Classics. Volume XV. Philadelphia: Westminster Press, 1961.

Miller, Arlyn. *Guidelines for Divorcing Parents*. Saluda, NC: Family Life Publication, Inc., 1979.

Niebuhr, H. Richard. *Christ and Culture*. New York: Harper and Row, 1951.

Nouwen, Henry. *The Wounded Healer*. New York: Image Books, Doubleday, 1990.

Oates, Wayne. *Pastoral Care and Social Problems*. Philadelphia: Westminster Press, 1975.

Olson, David H. and Blaine J. Flowers. "Predicting Marital Success and Prepare: A Predictive Validity Study." *Journal of Marital and Family Therapy*, October, 1986.

Pruyser, Paul. "The Master Hand." in *The New Shape of Pastoral Theology*. Nashville: Abingdon Press, 1969.

Sartre, Jean-Paul. *"No Exit" and Three Other Plays*. New York: Vintage Press, 1956.

Sinberg, Janet. *Divorce Is a Grown-Up Problem*. New York: Avon Books, The Hearst Corp., 1979.

Visher, Emily B. and John S. *Stepfamilies*. New York: Brunner/Mazel, 1979.

Westberg, Granger. *Good Grief.* Philadelphia: Fortress Press, 1971.

Wyse, Lois. Love *Poems for the Very Married.* New York: World Publishing Company, 1967.

ABOUT THE AUTHOR

Bruce R. Parmenter currently ministers with Christview Christian Church, St. Charles, MO. He is a Clinical Member and Approved Supervisor in the American Association For Marriage and Family Therapy.

Dr. Parmenter received his A.B. from Lincoln Christian Seminary, B.D. from Columbia Theological Seminary, S.T.M. from Christian Theological Seminary, and D.Min. in Pastoral Counseling from Eden Theological Seminary.

He was formerly a faculty member at Friends University in Marriage and Family Therapy, a member of the faculty of Lincoln Christian Seminary in Pastoral Counseling, and for twelve years the Director of Christian Counseling Centers, Inc., Champaign, IL.

Dr. Parmenter has published over 70 articles in *Seek Magazine*, *Christian Standard*, *The Lookout*, and *One Body Magazine*. He has written *The Healing of Our Grief* and *What the Bible Says About Self-Esteem*. Bruce and his wife, Judy, have five children and eleven grandchildren.